Prai   )son's

SWA   ...ucefully*

"The author definitely hits a nerve—and tickles the funny bone—with this essay collection."

December 2006 issue of *Southern Living*

"Thompson . . . has a knack for finding the Southern heart in ordinary life."

The Commercial Appeal—Memphis, Tennessee

"*SWAG* is a laugh-out-loud good time. . . . Southern women's lives are full of funny accounts of 'the rules,' but none comes funnier than Melinda Rainey Thompson's collection of essays, interspersed with 'how to' notes."

Clarion-Ledger—Clinton, Mississippi

"Thompson's collection of wry and witty essays . . . provides moments to make you laugh out loud, shed a few tears and stop and smell those roses—Southern roses, of course."

The Greenville Advocate—Greenville, Alabama

"Thompson produces a read that encourages one to look at all things in life with humor. . . . SWAG is a well-written account of being blessed to be both Southern and a woman—and all the trials and tribulations that go along with both."

Jackson Free Press—Jackson, Mississippi

Thomas and Cheryl Upchurch of Montgomery's bookstore, Capitol Book & News, state that *SWAG* is "the funniest book to come down the pike in some time. . . . Southern women of a certain age come into the store, pick this book up, and within a couple of seconds they're struggling to maintain their dignity when all they really want to do is laugh hysterically."

The Montgomery Advertiser—Montgomery, Alabama

The SWAG Life

Also by Melinda Rainey Thompson:
SWAG: Southern Women Aging Gracefully

The SWAG Life

Melinda Rainey Thompson

JOHN F. BLAIR
PUBLISHER
Winston-Salem, North Carolina

John F. Blair, Publisher

The paper in this book meets the guidelines for permanence and
durability of the Committee on Production Guidelines for Book
Longevity of the Council on Library Resources.

First Printing 2007

Cover Art
La Dee Dah by J D Adams, Invogueart

Design and composition by Angela Harwood

Library of Congress Cataloging-in-Publication Data

Thompson, Melinda Rainey, 1963-
The SWAG life / Melinda Rainey Thompson.
p. cm.
ISBN-13: 978-0-89587-351-4 (pbk. : alk. paper)
ISBN-10: 0-89587-351-6 (pbk. : alk. paper) 1. Women--Southern
States. 2. Middle-aged women--Southern States. 3. Women--Southern
States--Humor. I. Title.

HQ1438.S63T45 2007
305.244'20975--dc22
2007019125

For my boys, Warner and Nat, and for my
husband, Bill, especially. Also for my Papa,
with love

Contents

Preface

If you didn't read my first book, *SWAG: Southern Women Aging Gracefully*, you need to go out and buy it right now and read it. There are some important things in there that you need to know before moving on to this book. I'm not sure I can catch you up right here with just this preface.

The main thing you need to know is that the first book was an accident. I'm going about my ordinary, twenty-first-century Southern woman's life the same way you are. We've probably run into each other at the Piggly Wiggly, the ballpark, the church, the school, or out there in the errand-running of life. Even if we've never met personally, I bet we know some of the same people. The South is like that—connected in a way that is both comforting and a little frightening.

In August of 1998, I began writing a monthly newsletter out of my home because I was searching for intellectual stimulation to supplement my mind-numbing, hard, manual-labor job as a stay-at-home mom in the South. I wondered if other women were struggling with the same life questions I was, and I wanted to know if we were worrying about the same problems in different cities and states. Sometimes, I think the only differences in women all over the world are accents and geography. I thought it would make me feel sane, normal, and confident that I was making a difference in the world if I could just connect with the rest of you. You know what? It did.

My little writing hobby grew into a subscription list of thousands—a job way too big for my dining-room table. That's when I decided to write a book. When John F. Blair, Publisher, published *SWAG* in 2006, SWAGs like you came out to meet and welcome me in cities all over the South. I was stunned. I'll be forever grateful for those first readers. I have thoroughly enjoyed talking to every single one! I had the time of my life on the first book tour, and I still love to speak to groups of SWAGs all over the place—in between ball games, Brownie meetings, school programs, grocery shopping, and laundry duties. It's a zoo around here.

This second book, *The SWAG Life*, wasn't part of a grand plan, either. It just happened. My excuse is that writing is much cheaper than therapy, so I hope all of you continue to enjoy reading as much as I love writing because I'm having a ball. I'm here to tell you that writing is a good gig if you can get it.

Thanks to those of you who continue to read *SWAG: Southern Women Aging Gracefully* and to give it as gifts to your friends. My greatest writing accomplishment is not a royalty check. My proudest moments are when a woman tells me that she laughed out loud reading my book. My heart flips over in my chest every single time. It's like a two-margarita high. I hope you enjoy *The SWAG Life* every bit as much as you did the first book.

My eight-year-old daughter asked: "Mom, is the second book about the same stuff as your first book, all that standing in line and getting old, grownup stuff like that?" She never really thought the first book had a prayer for success without illustrations, a princess, magic, animals, or some other kind of hook. "Sequels are almost never as good as the original, Mama," she added.

"You're right," I told her, "but I gave this book a lot of thought, and I worked really hard on it." She looked supportive in an I-love-you-anyway-because-you're-my-mama way, but she didn't seem sold on the second-book idea. I have no doubt she will be checking my sales numbers on Amazon.com. For an eight-year-old, she's a particularly savvy consumer. I know one thing: all of you will certainly let me know whether or not you like the second book. All the SWAGs I've met are like my daughter—bossy.

I learned with the publication of my first book that there are many individuals in the world who think along the same lines I do. This fact was incredibly satisfying to discover because nothing makes me happier than finding other people who have the good sense to agree with me. I admit that a little personal validation makes my day. In an unexpected twist, I was surprised to find out how many non-SWAGs enjoy reading about all the things that we SWAGs get up to. I prefer to think that we are, indeed, breathtakingly fascinating individuals, but I admit there may be some freakshow spying going on, especially by the men who love us. Well, as my daughter would say, *whatever*.

We Southern women are what we are. We're a force of nature, a peculiar product of location, upbringing, disposition, and natural inclination. It's a volatile mix of nature and nurturing. Like women everywhere, we are often generous, philanthropic, kind, and fair. We can also be vain, narrow-minded, petty, and a teeny-tiny bit bossy. I know I mentioned that bossy trait earlier, but it probably wouldn't hurt to mention it again. It's encoded on the *XX* chromosome rather forcefully down here in the South. I bet it wouldn't take two seconds to map a genetic predisposition. On rare occasions, Southern women, like everyone, are just flat out wrong about something. My flat-out-wrong experiences are a constant source of writing inspiration. I once got a whole chapter out of a fruit tree that I didn't even know was growing in my own yard.

Although I happen to be the one paying attention and jotting down life's little ups and downs as they happen to me, I am well aware that it could just as easily be any one of you writing these essays. I am under no illusion that I am unique or special. I put on my control-top stockings the same way the rest of you do. The most common comment I hear at book signings is: "I feel like you're writing about my life!" I always say, "That's because I am!"

I want to thank all of the Southern women in my life—close friends and relatives, acquaintances, those I've met only once, and perfect strangers standing in line in front of me. (You'll read about that stranger-standing-in-line woman when you get to the "Mailing

Mama" essay in this book. You are not going to believe it. I'm not over that yet, and I wrote it.) Thanks to you, I always have plenty of material. The trick is figuring out how to use it without getting sued, shot, or socially shunned for the rest of my life. Luckily, most of the humor I write is at my own expense. My life is a deep well of character-building experiences for me and entertaining reading for you. I never know what lesson the Lord is going to have in store for me from week to week, but it's always a little adventure.

In my life, I've learned that, together, two women can take the most mundane of tasks and make them into something extraordinary. In a way, that's a wonderful gift and a blessing. It's a way of living that isn't dependent on money, good health, leisure time, or any other random variable. I swear that I have had fun with a friend while renewing a driver's license (you should have seen some of those ID pictures); in between bouts of throwing up (I threw up for months when I was pregnant with my first child—life had to go on); and picking out marble for my friend's fireplace. (That woman had to touch every piece of Alabama marble in the quarry before she could make up her mind. I was ravenous, and even though she doesn't eat enough to keep a hummingbird alive, I eat more like a buzzard, and I was ready to go to lunch.)

One of my biggest complaints about human beings is that most of us live for the highlights. It reminds me of adults who videotape their children's birthday parties, school pageants, and ball games. They're so busy recording those moments for posterity that they never actually enjoy them, or allow their kids to enjoy them, or they miss them entirely.

I think that real life is going on between all the high holy days. We all forget that sometimes. That's what I'm trying to capture in *The SWAG Life*, the exalted moments of heaven sandwiched right in the minutia of the daily grind. I find that most treasured moments usually happen at unexpected times—when there are unmade beds, unwashed dishes, and I'm wearing no makeup and have a fever blister. I'm learning to grab those moments with both hands, to be more spontaneous, to lighten up a little. I hope these pages provide you with some genuine belly laughs. They're free, and I think they're good for your soul—and mine.

Acknowledgments

A lot more work goes into publishing a book than you might think. When you get involved in the process, it's like discovering a whole new world. All I do is the writing, and, honestly, that's the easy part. As you might expect, I have a few people to thank:

First of all, thanks to Jake Reiss at the Alabama Booksmith in Homewood, Alabama, where I live. Jake was there from the beginning for me, and I'll never forget it.

Next, I want to acknowledge the incredible work of the John F. Blair staff. No writer could ever ask for a better relationship than I have experienced while working with them. The Blair staff proved to me that there are successful publishers out there who are honest, responsible, professional, courteous, kind, and a lot of fun. In particular, I thank: Carolyn Sakowski, Ed Southern, Kim Byerly, and most of all, my editor, Angela Harwood. They took a chance on an unknown writer, and I never want to let them down.

I want to thank SIBA and the independent booksellers across the South who welcomed me into their stores, hand-sold my book, and made a difference in its success.

Thank you to my mother, a woman who shares my sense of humor, travels with me at a moment's notice, baby-sits my children for me, bullies me into doing more than I think I can do, goes shopping with me when I have to wear something other than khakis and a T-shirt, and laughs with me about the little things. She's the kind of mother I wish everyone could have.

Thanks to my friends all across the South who turned out for book signings, took me out to lunch or dinner, allowed me to stay in their homes, or helped me find my way around their cities. A special thank you goes to "Hotel Fail" in Jackson, Mississippi, where cheese straws are always on offer. Most of all, thanks to friends like Phyllis, Tricia, Vivian, Laura, and Barbara who took on my book project as their own. There is nothing I would not do for my friends. I saw a greeting card once that said, "Friends help you move. Best friends help you move *bodies*." That sums it up perfectly for me.

Finally, to my family—parents, sister, aunts, cousins, and in-laws: thank you for supporting me. The biggest thank you of all to Bill and my children, my favorite people in the world.

The Suburban Cliché

The Suburban Cliché

As a Southern woman and a self-identified spokeswoman for my people, there are few things I detest more than being labeled a suburban cliché. No woman I know wants to be reduced to a stereotype. Too predictable. And boring.

Nothing ruffles my feathers faster than watching a stranger mentally adjust my intelligence quotient down a few points because I have a Southern accent and wear red lipstick. I have been known to reduce arrogant Yankee men to rubble with a few well-placed bits of conversational plastique without having to raise my voice or smudge my lipstick.

Although I admit to being a little defensive in this area, I assure you that no one has ever been on the receiving end of one of my put-downs unless he or she *really had it coming*. Over the years, I've been tempted to pin my graduate degree to a neck scarf to ensure a receptive audience in some intellectual quarters.

I've learned that being a physically small woman makes me appear to be a soft target to some people. Predictably, bullies and stupid people like to prey upon individuals smaller than they are. To that, I say: tell it to Condoleeza Rice, honey! Fortunately (or unfortunately, depending upon how you look at it), I've rather outgrown the petite physique of my youth, and now I am a mature woman of substance who can elbow her way into the heart of a department-store clearance sale with all the other suburban sharks.

Sadly, like you, I occasionally find myself suddenly and painfully aware that my life appears to be a stereotype in the silliest of ways, right when I least expect it. I find that such moments call for some spiritual introspection, lifestyle reevaluation, and thoughtful self-examination.

Stereotypes exist for a reason, of course. We all admit that. Mother-in-law jokes exist because of the frequency of mother-in-law problems. Those of us who are mothers worry about our children. All the time. We worry about everything—things we can control and things we can't, about important problems our children will face and about insignificant issues. We worry that our children will experiment with drugs or have to fight in a war. We also worry that they will go bald before they're thirty and that no one will ask them to dance at the prom. The truth is that no matter how much we would all like to be judged as individuals, we are all guilty of the occasional over-generalization.

At its best, a stereotype is a social shortcut, a sound bite to predict behavior, buying habits, or the reaction your child can expect after confessing that he left his winter coat at school *again*. We've all made those judgments—just and unjust—about others. It's when the labels are applied to us, personally, that life seems so terribly unfair.

Have you ever had a moment when you were suddenly forced by someone to view yourself from an outsider's point of view? It's a memorable and eye-opening experience. I can clearly recall a few such instances in my life. One that sticks out in my mind occurred on a typical afternoon, back in the days when I had three children under the age of five. On that day, we had numerous Play-Doh,

Lego, and coloring projects going on simultaneously when the objective observer, the telephone repairman, surveyed the room and asked me in a hushed, pity-filled voice, "Is it always like this?"

I was initially confused. "Like what?" I asked. As far as I was concerned, we were having a good day. Nobody had to go to the emergency room. Nothing of great financial or sentimental value had been broken beyond repair, and nobody was in trouble—a fairly successful parenting afternoon. In that split second, however, I was forced to step out of my own comfortable niche in life for a brief out-of-body experience to view my little family through the eyes of the (obviously) single, childless, twenty-something-year-old telephone repairman.

For the first time, the Batman outfit my son had been wearing for the past three days didn't look so adorable. It just looked dirty. A quick whiff of another child's diaper confirmed his desperate need for a clean, environmentally unfriendly, disposable diaper, and the cat toy I'd let the baby chew on seemed grounds for the state to remove my children from our happy home. The repairman's question had reduced my seemingly happy day to evidence of domestic squalor and parental neglect.

Another time I had one of those I-am-a-living-breathing-stereotype frights occurred recently. I was struggling to get my keys out of my purse to open the front door of my house when an aggressive magazine salesman pegged me as an easy mark all the way from the sidewalk. I watched him quickly scan my house, my car, my clothes, and the packages in my arms and sum me up, with an obnoxious smirk on his face, as the quintessential soccer mom, swing voter, suburban, Southern female cliché.

I have to admit that superficial appearances gave him a lot of ammunition (although I would argue that all the evidence against me was circumstantial). I had a huge bottle of orange-flavored vodka under one arm, and I was balancing a stack of men's dry cleaning while trying to dig my keys out of an expensive designer handbag (which I'd like to point out I've been using for the past fifteen years). In my other hand I was holding a small oil painting that I'd just had framed and two leaking Gatorade bottles that had been left in my car by eight-year-old baseball players.

I could see it in his eyes. I was about to become a victim of suburban profiling.

It wasn't the first time.

I can't explain why, but, suddenly, I felt the need to explain away my very existence to this stranger as if his opinion was in some way important to my life, and I had to take a deep breath to steel myself to sternly reject his sales offer.

Ever the well-mannered Southern woman, I tried the polite and dismissive, "No, thank you." When delivered in a freezing tone, these three words have been known to send amorous fraternity boys scurrying back to their cars. My well-delivered "no, thank you" has sent snooty waiters back to the dark corners of restaurants, but, alas, this salesman's skin was thicker than a swamp alligator's hide. He kept trying to angle his way around my dry cleaning to get between me and my front door. He was lucky I couldn't get to the panic button on my key chain without dropping the vodka.

"Come on, lady," he cajoled, "what else have you got to do today? Let me at least give you my pitch."

"Sorry," I replied, stepping inside, "I have an appointment to get my tongue pierced and then a meeting to attend at the United Nations. Flight leaves in an hour. Must rush."

In all honesty, I admit I rather enjoyed slamming the door in his face. Until then, I didn't know I had it in me. I've been warned my entire life that I am going to get killed one day because I am afraid to be rude.

All in all, I considered my encounter with the salesman to be a good day's work—another Southern stereotype crushed under my fashionable boots with time left over to sit on my porch swing, sip a little sweet tea, and touch up my lipstick before I had to pick up my children from school.

Exercise Guilt

"DON'T YOU JUST LOVE TO EXERCISE?" A SKINNY woman in black spandex and full makeup had the audacity to ask me before six o'clock in the morning.

"No," I responded.

The poor woman was so stunned that she tripped on her treadmill and had to grab the armrests and swing her legs wildly to the side to recover.

"As a matter of fact, I hate it," I said to that sanctimonious, well-toned, perky wench who had the misfortune to choose an exercise machine near my own.

"Well, at least you're here," she said, "that counts for something."

"I am here," I reflected, "because I do not wish to die an untimely death."

"A lot of that has to do with genetics," she replied, as if this was breaking news.

"Yes, I know, and the cheeseburgers and chocolate don't help. Really, I'm just hedging my bets, kind of like soldiers who find religion in a foxhole," I expanded on my theory.

I really don't like to sweat. I despise showering twice before lunch. I abhor walking around and around a track like a donkey in harness.

At least once a year, I find myself thinking up excuses to skip my exercise routine. "Just this once," I say. "I'll think about it tomorrow," I argue with Scarlett O'Hara logic. Usually, this procrastination begins legitimately with a sick child or a genuine scheduling conflict. Somehow, though, once I've allowed myself a single excused absence, I find it easier and easier to avoid the three-times-a-week exercise grind until finally I'm playing hooky if it's Groundhog Day or I can't find my favorite workout clothes. Pitiful.

My dirty little secret is that I don't like to exercise. There. I've said it out loud. I know it's not fashionable to say so, but before you get all sanctimonious on me, please take note that I exercise anyway. Like most good-for-me activities, the real reasons I exercise are guilt and fear. I want my kids to be healthy, so I have to set a good example, darn it. Honestly, the things I do for my children. Yes, I have more energy (blah, blah, blah), and, yes, I feel good about myself afterwards—a lot like the feeling I get when I finally clean out my closet or mop the patio. Although I feel guilty when I don't exercise, I've never felt that intense pleasure some of my fitness-freak friends talk about. Really, I just exercise so I won't feel guilty about not exercising. Plus, I'm nothing if not nauseatingly responsible.

Occasionally, however, I fall off the exercise wagon, and although I always eventually claw my way back up, sometimes I just lie there in the mud and mull over my options for a few minutes. I've had some fairly heated debates with myself regarding exercise. One of the questions that keeps popping in my mind is: What would be so bad about being old and fat?

I've given this some thought. The first catch is that you have to live long enough to *be* old, right? Let's say I exercise regularly for the rest of my life, and so that buys me, maybe, another year of life than I'd live otherwise if I just ate Krispy Kreme doughnuts and read books on my sofa. Let's say I worked out all those years three times a week for an hour each time. Since there are fifty-two weeks in the year, that would be 156 hours spent in the gym every year multiplied by however many years I have left on the big roll up yonder. Looks like I could either give up that last year now, at the outset of middle age, forget exercising altogether, and do fun things. Or, alternatively, I could waste an equal amount of time little by little over the years attending whatever exercise class is currently in style. What kind of trade-off is that?!

I'm still looking for a third option.

I try to listen to my body since it has served me well so far. I can remember a time when my instincts said, "RUN!" when a creepy guy got on the elevator with me. I did, and I'm still convinced he was up to no good. I always knew when I was pregnant before a test confirmed it, and I knew when I had strep throat even though two throat cultures said I didn't. (That nurse was plenty apologetic when she called to tell me there'd been a mix-up with patient names.) My body rarely tells me to exercise. Oh, it might encourage me to go for a leisurely walk around the block, but I've never heard it mutter a thing about treadmills or tummy crunches.

My body says things like:

"What are we doing on this stationary bike? We're not even going anywhere!

"Let's get a book and some candy and stretch out on the porch swing and read. That'd be fun!

"Do we want to get all hot and sweaty and have to take another shower before noon?

"Since when are we drinking plain old water? Honey, nothing should be squirted into this mouth from a plastic bottle at our age. Put some liquor in this water, and we'll talk.

"Who put all these diet drinks in the refrigerator?"

Lately, I'd say my body has been a bad influence on me. For years, it did everything I told it to—immediately—no creaking, groaning, or slow response times. Until I turned forty, I could eat anything I wanted without the slightest increase in weight or cholesterol level, and I did.

I liked that.

When that little party ended, I felt like an over-tired two-year-old being put down for a nap. I was mad with everyone and everything in sight. Suddenly, for the first time ever, my waistline was spreading; my legs were jiggling; my eyesight was failing; my hair was graying; my face was falling; and it was all happening so fast that I was afraid parts of my aging body might fall off like an old muffler as I walked down the street.

That's what motivated me to start exercising regularly: fear, guilt, and *vanity*. Now that I think about it, these three human emotions have been used for centuries to govern entire populations. I guess they're as good reasons as any for me to exercise.

The New Mattress

I FIRMLY BELIEVE THAT WE SHOULD ALL TRY SOMETHING new every twenty years or so. Today, I bought a new king-sized mattress. You might not think that is something I'd be inspired to write about, but you'd be wrong. I've already written about a previous prosaic purchase, my laundry hamper, and if I could come up with a fitting elegy (that's pretty hard to do; just try it), I'd write about my twentieth anniversary present, my all-time favorite appliance: my ice machine. I rank that ice machine up there with opera-length pearls and contact lenses as the top three finest presents I have ever received.

I'm an ice freak. I can tell you what kind of ice—cubed, large or small, half-moon or full-moon shaped, or crushed—is served in every restaurant I patronize on a regular basis. Ice matters to me. It can make or break my dining experience. For example, I might say, "I don't want to go there. They don't have good ice," or, equally irritating, in my opinion, "they don't put enough ice in their glasses." I'm embarrassed to voice such a provincial, small-minded prejudice, but the room-temperature-beverage deal is enough to turn me off to the entire European continent. I like to visit, but I couldn't live there, always having to ask for ice and then more ice when they bring out two stingy pieces. I am a woman who knows and is comfortable with her own limitations.

I like to start every day with a tall Styrofoam cup filled with small cubes of ice. (These cups can be reused several times; they are top-rack dishwasher safe, in case you didn't know. I do not want to hear about the evils of Styrofoam. I love Styrofoam.) I actually prefer crushed ice, but, for some inexplicable reason, it's almost impossible to get a freestanding crushed-ice machine for residential use. I'd be happy to purchase the kind of icemaker you'd normally see in a hotel kitchen, but no one seems interested in selling one to me. Every time a plumber comes to my home to fix something, I ask about icemakers. Over the years, I've been the recipient of a confusing jumble of excuses associated with old pipes and my eighty-year-old home that ultimately boil down to a big "no" on the crushed-ice machine. Rest assured I have not given up on crushed ice. Technology improves every day. If we can get email in outer space, I just know somebody can get crushed ice in my kitchen in Alabama.

Now that I've gotten that little ice digression out of the way, I want to get back to the mattress discussion.

I had no idea that buying a new mattress would be such a life-changing event. The mattress my husband and I have been sleeping on is about twenty years old, but it looks eighty. We were both in graduate school and poor as church mice when we bought it, so it didn't exactly start out as a top-of-the-line purchase, and now it looks dog-eared and tired, like a worn-out library book whose pages have grown soft, or a child's teddy bear that has had its fur loved off over the years.

Even with all the pillows and bedding disguising the worst of the wear, our old bed looks war-defeated and down at the mouth. If it could figure out a way to hoist a white pillowcase, it would probably surrender to the mattress gods. It reminds me of an old residential neighborhood that has just about given in to commercial property owners. Our bed looks like the sagging front stoop of an old house that is propped up between a new gas station and a taco stand. Our mattress started out its life shaped like a traditional rectangle, but now it reminds me of a shaky rectangle a preschooler might draw with a fat crayon.

There are two hollowed-out troughs on each side of our mattress where you might imagine two pot-bellied pigs have wallowed. To put it more delicately, my husband and I have, literally, carved out our own particular niches. All the way across the bottom, the foot of the bed slopes toward the floor because all three of our children routinely turn one somersault and bounce on their bottoms on the end of the bed before finding their feet and exiting our bedroom after early morning greetings.

When we pulled the old mattress off the bedframe, I was startled to see that even the metal bedframe's legs were bent, so the castors sit sideways, at odd angles, drunkenly askew, looking for all the world like a child who attempted to turn a cartwheel and landed unexpectedly with elbows and knees in unlikely places.

Underneath the mattress, I found: two pairs of reading glasses, a small plastic pirate, a hair ribbon, two marbles, and a wooden baseball bat my husband keeps handy to intimidate burglars. (We're not a gun-owning kind of family.) I guess we can safely assume we're not descended from royalty like the princess in "The Princess and the Pea." Heck, if there had been a black-eyed pea under there, somebody around here would have probably eaten it. There was also an embarrassing assortment of candy wrappers, cat hair, and single socks just hanging out under our old mattress like it was visiting day at the old folks' home.

Mattresses are expensive. If you haven't bought one in a long time, let me tell you the prices are going to come as something of a shock to you. I spent an entire year working up the nerve to write a fat check for that sinful amount of money, and really, I was only persuaded to part with the cash when the choice became new mattress or back surgery.

You'd have thought I was waiting for the Publisher's Clearing House prize patrol the day my mattress was scheduled for delivery. I watched for the delivery van from my porch as diligently as a lifeguard with binoculars spotting sharks. When the delivery man telephoned from his truck to ask for directions, I promised to stand in my front yard and wave him into the driveway like an air-traffic controller. I had my cell phone, a pink handkerchief, a Styrofoam cup full of ice, and I was determined to bring that truck into my driveway safely.

I could tell by the expressions on the faces of the delivery-men that they were a little shocked by the state of my old mattress. I asked if they could haul it away for me, and they said, "Yes, ma'am . . . we haven't seen one of these in a *while*." They seemed to find my mattress an object of some interest—like a museum piece, perhaps. Just out of curiosity, I asked what they did with the old mattresses, and they said, "Well, usually, we just dump 'em at the loading docks, and somebody'll pick 'em up, but I don't know with this one. . . ." It was obvious they didn't think anybody would be tempted to steal my old mattress.

I didn't care a bit. I was way too busy hoisting myself up (mattresses are much, much taller these days) and lying full-length and spread eagle (think *The Da Vinci Code* here) on my new mattress before those men could even head back down my stairs.

"You gone go ahead and try it out now, huh?" they asked.

"You better believe it!" I answered. "I've been looking forward to this for a long time!" I told them. "Look on the kitchen counter on your way out. I cut a piece of pound cake for each of you. I think this new mattress calls for a celebration!" I added.

"Yes, ma'am," they responded, a little warily, I thought, for men who have just been tipped with two big slices of homemade pound cake.

I heard one of the men tell the other one just before the screen door slammed: "I been deliverin' mattresses for thirty years, and I aint never seen nobody more excited to get a mattress than that 'un."

He got that right.

Remote Power

WE HAVE SEVENTEEN REMOTE-CONTROL DEVICES floating around our home. That is a ridiculous, embarrassing admission—like bragging about how many cheese curls you can eat or how big your *Soap Opera Digest* collection is. Even worse: that's just the number of remotes I could spot when I stormed through my house today counting them in a fit of remote-controlled rage. Out of the seventeen I found, not one was the one I was actually searching for, naturally. We probably have more than seventeen remotes because I can recall a few more that have gone AWOL over the years.

Theoretically, as you know, these devices are used to control the assorted electronic umbilical cords that connect our family to the rest of the world. You would think we lived on some remote island or snowbound glacier instead of a conveniently located suburb of our state's largest city. My husband and children seem to find them handy. Of course, these are the same people who text-message each other about football games they are watching in different rooms in the same house. What idiots.

Unfortunately, remote-control units don't work for me. I point. I click. I even wave the remotes theatrically up and down and side to side *while* pointing and clicking. Even so, nine times out of ten, I get nothing in response—no magical red laser light dances to my bidding. I'm beginning to take it personally.

I firmly believe that inanimate bits of technology can sense those of us who don't know what we're doing. I'm convinced that the computer geeks who design remote-control devices love playing with the minds of technologically challenged people like me. I figure one of the highlights of their day is writing a few lines of computer code just to mess with us. They entertain themselves by visualizing us frantically pointing and clicking in vain. Those computer geeks snicker to themselves because only they know the remotes have been designed to work against us. Eventually, we scream. We throw our remote controls to the far corners of our sofas or whack them on the tops of coffee tables until they splinter into pieces.

It's not pretty being a technological moron.

Open any bedside or end-table drawer in my house, and you'll find a pile of remote controls in all sizes and shapes. In between sofa cushions, underneath heavy pieces of furniture, in the pockets of winter coats, in the depths of toy chests—you'll find more remote controls. They're everywhere—like an infestation of bed bugs.

I am ashamed to confess that we have remote controls for items we don't even own anymore. That's right. Appalling, isn't it? Somehow, these remotes have become separated from the items they once enabled, and because I don't really know for certain if they are superfluous, I'm afraid to throw them away. Someday I may need them. There's nothing actually wrong with them; it's just that they have—through no fault of their own—been inadvertently estranged from their better halves. This explains the outdated, useless remotes that suck up valuable table-top, shelf, and junk-drawer space in my house.

The most offensive remote of all is the mystery remote. You know the one I mean. I'm talking about the remote-control device that no member of the family remembers owning. This remote has never, to anyone's best recollection, controlled anything we have ever owned. It is possible, even, that it is merely a visiting remote that migrated in someone's pocket and later established residency through an adverse possession loophole.

I don't know of a single girlfriend who can tell you at a glance, off the top of her head, with any degree of certainty, which remote controls which item in her house. Like a sailor on an aircraft carrier trying to guide a pilot in for a night landing, I routinely pick up three or four remotes and point them enthusiastically and hopefully toward some mute piece of equipment that I want to turn on until I see something light up in response to all my flailing around. Like a gleeful toddler, I push buttons with no regard to consequences in search of a change in programming, volume, or power. Occasionally, I get lucky, but it's just like a chimpanzee taking the SAT test. Eventually, the chimp is bound to get one or two chemistry questions right.

The proliferation of remote-control devices in ordinary households like mine reflects an insidious cultural shift. These days, you don't have to actively pursue remote-control ownership. They're served up automatically like fast-food-meal deals in the bottom of Styrofoam and bubble wrap with every new electronic purchase.

All of the new technology I'm referring to is, of course, out of date by the time it debuts in our living rooms. In fact, the world of high-tech toys, appliances, and office equipment changes so fast that their entire life span from foreign-country computer chip to American landfills is less than two years or so. Pretty soon, the average Ziploc baggie is going to have a longer life span than what we can expect out of our cell phones.

Have you noticed that no one fixes electronic items anymore? The most famous television repair shop my city ever had is now a trendy eatery. Even if you find someone who will attempt a repair job—just out of principle and the desire to avoid environmental waste—nine times out of ten it's cheaper to buy a new item. Plus, we've now become so dependent upon the technology crutches in our lives that we can't do without them long enough to have them repaired. I'm sure you've stood behind someone in line who can't get off his or her cell phone long enough to order a cup of coffee. It seems like just a few years ago astronauts had to wait to get to the other side of the moon before checking in with Houston.

Kind of makes you think, doesn't it?

Ten Ways You Know You Live in the Suburbs

1) The squirrels, birds, raccoons, and other wild animals look fatter, happier, and healthier than most humans you know.

2) You call the wrong telephone number and wind up talking to a perfect stranger about spring soccer registration for ten minutes.

3) Your children call the police officers and fire fighters by name.

4) Every kid on the block knows which tree in your yard is home base.

5) When you go shopping, you don't have to worry about finding a parking space. You can always park in the driveway of a friend who lives nearby.

6) Your children know which bank, grocery store, and dry cleaner gives out free lollipops.

7) Your grocery store will deliver bottled water, diapers, and Gatorade by the case.

8) You accidentally leave your purse at home when you go to the drugstore, and they tell you to pay for it the next time you come in.

9) The ice-cream man knows which ice-cream selections your child isn't allowed to purchase because of his allergies.

10) If you leave your child at the football stadium, you know another kid's parents will bring him home.

A Woman With a Past

Ghosts of Boyfriends Past

IT NEVER FAILS. *IF YOU WEAR IT, THEY WILL COME*—JUST when you don't want them to come. That's right. On the one day of your entire life when you rush out of your house wearing the first item of clothing you can grab to cover your nakedness, when you forgo even a smidgeon of makeup, when your hair is unwashed and sticking out in all directions, you will run into an old boyfriend within fifteen minutes.

This is a statistical fact. Ninety-nine percent of the time, I'm fully dressed, hair brushed, war paint applied, appropriately (occasionally stylishly) clothed by 7 AM every morning. I have three children, so my one shot at the shower is before they're awake. I've found that if I wait until later, I never get around to it. If I go to exercise at 8 AM, it's likely I'll still be in exercise clothes at 3 PM. The truth is that once I climb on the day's escalator, there's just no easy way to jump off. There are no detours, no forks in the road on the escalator. It's a one-way deal, up or down, and all I take with me is what I can haul around in a shopping basket and a purse.

Because I'm usually so painfully organized—beds made, laundry started, and list in hand—I find it particularly demeaning and a grossly unfair representation of my character when I'm caught unprepared. No one should be judged on one bad-hair day. Don't you agree?

No one ever comes to visit unexpectedly right after I've cleaned the bathrooms or polished the silver. Never. Friends pop in to use the guest bathroom only when I've completely run out of toilet paper or the kids have left toothpaste snakes in the sink. No one walks into my kitchen to pour a drink when I have candles lighted and monogrammed cocktail napkins out. *Oh, no.* My unexpected kitchen guests always descend when I've left a big, smelly Fry Daddy on the counter to cool, or we're out of napkins and have been forced to use the extras that come with the Krispy Kreme doughnuts, or there are sticky, glittery valentines spread out on the counter in between the kids' breakfast dishes, which have congealed leftover oatmeal that looks like mud slides in California.

A certain amount of self-consciousness is natural, I think, when friends pop in, but, for some reason, I often feel the need to apologize for my life with excuses like, "I was just about to clean that up." It's bad enough to be caught off guard by your friends, but nothing, and I mean nothing, is more humiliating than being caught looking your worst by an old boyfriend.

If the fates, those three horrible old hags, must, for their own private amusement, throw an old boyfriend across my path, I'd like to look my best. I don't expect to look twenty years younger or anything, but I'd like to have my fat tummy nicely camouflaged under a well-cut jacket (I can afford nicer clothes now), my hair freshly dyed, with enough makeup applied to remind people where my eyes, cheeks, and lips are approximately located. I have modest goals. If I were a house, I wouldn't try to pass as Windsor Castle, but a comfortable cottage in the country with old roses and a leaky roof would be about right.

My most recent ghosts-of-boyfriends-past experience was typical. I could tell before I opened my eyes that morning that it was going to be one of those days. I had that swollen-face allergy feeling like I'd had three margaritas with salt at bedtime even though I hadn't. My children were slow getting up as if I was sending them off to a leprosy colony rather than the local, blue-ribboned school. One child remembered, as we were walking out the door, that he was supposed to bring two-dozen cookies shaped like fractions with him to school, and my daughter was determined to wear red Dorothy shoes and a football jersey and wanted me to help her pick out a "matching" hair bow. As an official "bow head" of the South, she knew the outfit was up to her, but the bow was non-negotiable. Needless to say, I didn't have time for a shower.

I slapped a piece of pound cake down on the counter in front of each child and called it breakfast (to their undisguised delight) and decided I could probably get away with throwing a raincoat over my pajamas to run the kids to school in the car.

That was my first mistake.

After grabbing my car keys and dark sunglasses, I loaded everyone up, offered various pieces of advice, encouragement, and threats to get my children through the day, kissed them goodbye at the crosswalk, and headed home.

Unlocking the front door and throwing my keys on the mantel, I was immediately distracted by the parched potted fern in my living room and decided to give it a drink before tackling anything else. After watering it at the kitchen sink, I realized it needed to drain a few minutes outside, and since it was still drizzling rain, I rolled up my pajama pants legs so they wouldn't drag in the mud.

I'd bought these flannel beauties strictly for lounging. They were rock-bottom priced, end-of-the-season ugly, but I didn't care because *no one would ever see them*. They were lime green, and they had pink fairies on them waving wands with stars coming out. Also, the only size left was large, so I had them folded over at the waist a couple of times. No bra, of course, and although I knew the top was buttoned improperly, I remind you that I was in a hurry. My feet were cold, so I had on white running socks beneath the turned-up pants bottoms. My shoes were upstairs in my bedroom closet, and since it was wet outside, I slipped on my oldest son's black, plastic pool shoes for the quick dash to the porch. They almost fit.

My hair was uncombed, and I have naturally curly hair, so . . . it's kind of hard to describe. I had on no makeup except traces of yesterday's artistry that had not been properly removed the night before. I hadn't made it to contact lenses yet, so I was sporting glasses that were approximately ten years out of date.

I hope you're getting a colorful mental picture here. I don't want to leave out a single painful detail that would prevent you from appreciating the depths of my personal humiliation.

I decided against the umbrella. Why bother? With my left hand I picked up the bag of dirty cat litter that needed to go out to the garbage, and with my right hand I opened the door and manhandled the potted fern out to drip dry when I, quite literally, bumped into my old boyfriend who was standing outside my back door, note in hand, ready to tuck a carefully phrased missive into my letter box.

I'd like to say that because I am such a mature, self-confident adult, I was able to laugh off the awkward moment and breeze my way through the encounter with witty conversation, but that would be lying. In fact, I was so horrified I couldn't think of a single thing to say. I had trouble remembering the old boy's name.

I must give credit where credit is due and say that after his face initially revealed the shell shock of one confronted by a former love who has, apparently, been turned into a hag from hell by the passing years, his expression never revealed another glimpse of the horror he must have felt at being treated to an early morning freak show.

"I see I may have come at an inconvenient moment," he said in that classic, understated Southern-male manner, but I could see the corners of his eyes crinkling with laughter, and I remembered, for the first time in years, how much I loved that.

"I'm glad to see that you still have nice manners," I said. "Come in, and I'll give you a piece of pound cake and a cup of coffee while I change out of my good-fairy pajamas."

Notes on Southern Men

Sometimes, it takes a Southern woman to translate the true meaning of a Southern man's sentences. It helps if she's known him for a while. The following is a list of expressions frequently used by Southern men, and their translations, which could easily be misunderstood by readers who are unfamiliar with the nuances of the language.

When a Southern man says that he "appreciates the tenor of your thoughts."
Translation: He knows you're mad; he just doesn't care.

On a less formal note, when he says that he knows "where you are coming from."
Translation: Same as above.

If he says he is "as disappointed as you are about the way things turned out."
Translation: He bears no personal responsibility for making you mad.

If he says that he "wouldn't hurt you for the world."
Translation: He is about to deliver a deathblow.

When asked to explain himself, if a Southern male recites a charming, meaning-of-life parable or invites you to amble down memory lane with him.
Translation: He has no intention of revealing a single useful bit of information.

If he explains that "no one worked harder than I to prevent this."

Translation: Nothing about this is his fault. He is actually a victim of an act of God, the capricious hand of fate, Lady Luck, the economy, or a vast right- or left-wing conspiracy.

When a Southern man tells you to call on him "at any time, if you need anything," and he'll "always be available to you." Translation: He is about to change his home and cell numbers, and his secretary at work has instructions not to put your calls through.

If he says that he "feels your pain," but he wants to be clear that he shares no personal responsibility for any relationship fallout. Translation: This is his story, and he's sticking to it.

When caught in a seemingly undeniable lie, a Southern man will explain that he has not really lied at all; he is merely a victim of "unforeseeable circumstances." Translation: The situation is a lot like a natural disaster where he, a chivalrous Southern gentleman, has had to make hasty and complicated choices that have resulted in unavoidable collateral damage to you. Bottom line: you are not going to see a penny from this man.

If he suggests that the "real problem is you." Translation: He had no idea you actually expected him to keep his word.

The Outfit

Do you have an all-time favorite article of clothing, something you've refused to give away even though you haven't been able to wear it for years? I do. It would not surprise me a bit to learn, if you interviewed a hundred little old ladies, that each one of them could lucidly recount the satisfying perfection of a day long ago when she was at the top of her game, fashion-wise. At that moment in time, the planets were aligned to show off her particular brand of beauty. Her beloved was behaving himself; the weather was fine, and she was granted an all-around good-hair day by the coiffeur gods. Best of all, she was almost drunk with an awareness that she was wearing her most stunning outfit. That ensemble was so flattering, slimming, and generally appealing that heads turned (men and women alike) from every direction to watch her sashay into the room.

Sadly, a woman only gets one or two of those moments in her whole life, unless she's been kissed by a genetic good fairy, but the occasional random fashion success can happen at any age. For example, I defy anyone who has ever seen a two-year-old proudly model sparkly, new, ruby-red Dorothy shoes or a big-girl white fur muff to an appreciative audience to argue that the heady euphoria of a successful fashion statement is limited to model-thin grown-ups. Certainly, little girls who have the hutzpa to accompany their mothers to the grocery store dressed in full, Snow White costume regalia (for the apple scene reenactment in the produce aisle, of course) richly deserve their fifteen minutes of fame and any ensuing rounds of spontaneous applause.

Imagine a woman in the Roaring Twenties, spinning away under the twinkling lights of a chandelier, clad in an exquisitely beaded flapper dress. After she dies, that flapper dress might be the one outfit her children find wrapped carefully in tissue paper and saved in the top of her closet—not with the fond hope that anyone will ever wear it again but because every few years, when she unwrapped the dress and shook it out in front of her, she could still smell the lingering scent that was her signature fragrance in her youthful heyday. She had only to feel the silky material fall through her fingers to remember herself and her friends as young, healthy, and full of fun. In that outfit, for that moment in time, that woman was heart-stoppingly beautiful, and, more importantly, perhaps, she *felt* beautiful, light on her feet, completely at ease in her skin.

I'm wearing my favorite outfit right now. (Well, technically, I'm still holding out for the full-length, black velvet opera cape which has yet to come my way, along with some romantic destination to justify its purchase since, in all honesty, I've never seen anyone wear a black velvet opera cape to the PTO meetings or anywhere else I usually go.) I like this outfit well enough to be buried in it, and I consider that to be the ultimate test as to whether or not an outfit is "the one" defining piece of clothing for a year, decade, or even a lifetime.

I'll just tell you right out—quite baldly—that I have on black velvet overalls. This, I tell you, is an outfit that could fulfill every woman's fashion fantasy. I should explain that I have a longstanding love affair with overalls. Before you wrinkle your nose in disgust, please credit me with a little taste. These are not Farmer Brown's overalls. Certainly not! All the overalls I have ever bought are cut lovingly to flatter a woman, and denim is not on my parade-of-hits list. I have snug, ribbed, corduroy overalls, high-tech, Tencel-fiber overalls, and lighter-than-air linen overalls. Right now, I have a little flirtation going on with a pair of antique-toile overalls that cost more than my last dental work. Although I haven't yet succumbed to their siren's song, I can tell you I'm watching those overalls like a chicken hawk for signs of a sale.

When I first spotted these black velvet overalls in the window of a small boutique, I was on an out-of-town trip with my husband. As every woman knows, money you spend while on vacation isn't real money until the credit-card bill arrives in the mail after you return home, so I wasn't concerned by minor budgetary constraints. I stopped dead on the sidewalk at the vision of these overalls, and I swear I heard strains of the Hallelujah chorus in my ears. Who could have imagined it? Overalls, my favorite piece of apparel, combined with my favorite fabric: black velvet. Together at last. One happy outfit. The marriage of black velvet and overalls is my personal clothing dream, kind of like marrying the man I adore and having him just happen to look like Pierce Brosnan's identical twin.

Imagine a pair of overalls that need not be confined to the garden, the park, or Sunday afternoon rambles around a flea market. These overalls are hip, chic even, and they cry out (I can hear it) for expensive, trendy jewelry and big-city, ultra-fab shoes that cost the earth.

Overalls, in my opinion, offer one of life's most perfect opportunities to combine total comfort with the richness of fine fabrics, jewelry, and accessories, and if you pay attention, you'll notice that a fully grown woman who is comfortable wearing overalls in public is a woman who can go the distance with you in a relationship. This is a woman who can drink cocktails with you on your porch all afternoon and still fill out your tax forms for you that night.

In case you haven't spent as much time thinking about overalls as I have, the first premise you must grasp is the secret attraction of overalls—for toddlers and adults: they don't actually touch your body anywhere except for the button closures on the shoulder. Therefore, the entirely unique beauty of overalls is that you can let it all hang out tummy-wise without feeling guilty or looking like an old beer-drinking sorority girl gone to seed. In addition, I feel compelled to let you in on a little secret I discovered myself. Although this is a slightly more indelicate detail than I usually share, the truth is that you don't actually have to wear a bra underneath your overalls if you aren't too generously endowed in the bosom department, and no one will ever know! Isn't that perfectly lovely?

Before I'd even signed my name on the credit-card receipt for those overalls, I'd already fantasized about being able to go out to a restaurant in my new outfit. Free at last! Imagine ordering without regard to confining clothing. All the way back to the car, I blessed the swanky Yankee designer who thought up this sinful little overall number. Secretly, I vowed that if these overalls survived their first trip to the dry cleaners, I'd get that designer's studio address off the Internet and write her a thank-you note extolling the virtues of her brilliant notion of combining overall comfort with black velvet.

The discovery of my black velvet overalls confirms what I've always suspected. The fashion industry spends billions trying to convince otherwise sane and logical women like me that to appear attractive, we simply must wear pointy-toed shoes set on circus-like stilts and other strange garments that only look appealing on six-foot-tall, underfed runway models who boast the unrealistic body measurements of Barbie. The old maxim of "vanity over comfort" is a theory I have never been able to whole-heartedly endorse. I can almost hear my clotheshorse of a mother saying, as she has so many times, "Take an aspirin before you go out for the evening! It'll be worth it. You look great in that outfit. I don't *care* if you're comfortable or not. *That's not the point!*"

I've discovered that if you look hard enough and often enough through the piles of expensive rags labeled high fashion, every designer creates at least one or two gems, and one of them may be the outfit you'll remember for the rest of your life or, at the very least, an outfit that won't embarrass you in public.

Things You Just Can't Say

THIS IS GOING TO COME AS NEWS TO SOME PEOPLE, and they are, frankly, just the people who need to hear it most. Here is the SWAG life lesson of the day: There are some things you just can't say. It doesn't matter if the situation is just crying out for them to be said. It doesn't matter if you injure one of your important internal organs trying to keep those words from flying out of your mouth. And, of course, it doesn't matter if what you want to say is the gospel truth. The truth is only going to help you if you're looking for an absolute defense in a libel suit; it will rarely help you out in regular life. It can get you into a heap of trouble faster than anything.

You can't say, "Your husband is cheating on you," for example. No matter what happens—whether the couple gets a divorce, or they make up, once again, and live happily ever after—you will forever after be the one who told them the bad news that everyone in town knew, but only you had the audacity to address. You will become the tainted friend.

Sadly, your self-righteous, tattletale behavior of inserting yourself into a situation that was none of your business in the first place will become more interesting gossip than the lying, adulterous spouse's behavior! Trust me. If the couple makes it through the bad patch in their marriage, you can count on the one thing that will unite them forever: neither one will like you one bit.

You can never unsay words that have big consequences. Once you've fired the conversational equivalent of a shoulder-launched missile, collateral damage is inevitable. Sentences like, "I think you should divorce him" are so weighty that once they're thrown out there in the world, nothing can ever go back to the way it was before those words were uttered. Once you've said, "Your daughter dresses like a prostitute," there's really no way to tone that down. Neither you nor the mother of the inappropriately dressed daughter will ever forget those words, no matter how much everyone involved might wish they could. There is no magic time machine to take you back to the moment before you said, "I thought you knew they were fake."

There is nothing more dangerous to a circle of friends than a woman who never has an unexpressed thought. We've all known at least one of these women. These women are usually well intentioned, but they just can't help themselves. They have to butt in. It's just like watching a puppy think. You can read the thoughts racing across a puppy's face like a stock-market ticker: "Oooh, I want that porkchop on the table. If I grab that porkchop, I'm going to be in sooo much trouble, but it looks so juicy, *I don't think I can help myself!*" Well. We all know the inevitable conclusion. The porkchop is history. The dog is in deep doo-doo.

Let me point out the obvious. We are not dogs. We are supposed to be more evolved than dogs. We all have to consider the consequences of our words a long, long time before we scatter them out into the cosmos like sparks from an evil fairy's wand. When you are tempted to spew forth some big truth, I urge you to spend a few minutes in self-examination. Why do you want to share this earth-shattering information? Are your motives pure? Will anything at all be helped by your words? Making yourself feel better does NOT count.

What in the world makes you think you are the person to tell this news? Are you a trained psychiatrist or counselor, or are you a scary, self-righteous, holier-than-thou tattletale who always thinks you have a duty to pass along gossip? Lord save us from people trying to help us. Bumbling, well-intentioned do-gooders who stomp right in where angels fear to tread have to be one of the most dangerous species on earth. My personal motto is: if in doubt, don't! I tell you, that philosophy has saved me a world of worry. Feel free to adopt it as your own. Unless you have a passport stamped with the words "Divine Prophet" as your occupation, it pays to check and double check to make sure you are the right man or woman for the job. Odds are you're not.

Most importantly: have you been *asked* for your opinion? We all know how much free advice is worth. Has anyone knocked on your door and begged you for your pearls of wisdom like you're the Dali Lama on some mountaintop in Tibet? If not, you need to go home and attend to your own business because you are just going to get yourself and everybody around you in a heap of trouble. It's like watching the cast in a scary movie as they investigate the mysterious sounds in the basement. You want to save them all the way from your movie-theater seat. "Wait! Don't go down there! Get out of the house!" you urge them. Do they ever listen? No, they do not.

Unfortunately, and this is the tricky part, it is also true, on very rare occasions, that someone does have to be the truth teller. These occasions are few and far between and usually involve someone potentially dying if no one has the guts to step up to the plate and tell it like it is. For example, if your friend's husband literally beats the daylights out of her, well, then you let fly with whatever words or frying pans are necessary to get that woman out of her house and into your guest room.

I've come up with one reliable rule of thumb to help all of us Southern women decide if we are called upon to tell big-time truths out loud. Here it is: Have you ever sucked on the same pacifier as this woman? If the answer is yes, then you've got a solid friendship that goes back to the cradle, and it is possible that this might be your sticky wicket to either go through or around. Still, think long and hard before you tell your friend something you may need DNA evidence to prove. Remember, if you say those words out loud, there's no going back.

In addition, any derogatory truths you are tempted to voice about a woman's mother, sister, children, or husband should be examined carefully to see if there is any loophole to excuse you from this job. There are no circumstances in which you should agree with your friend that her children are horribly behaved. I repeat: it doesn't matter if this is true, and everyone in town knows it. Your role is simply to listen to your friend vent about her children's transgressions, to make helpful suggestions if you think she is really serious about discipline this time, or to offer excuses for her children's misbehavior that will make your friend feel better. You might say her kids were tired, cranky, had too much candy, or were egged on by some other child's antics. If you're lucky, those kids will eventually go to college or prison. After that, you'll buy them wedding gifts and never have to fool with them again. In the end, you'll still have your friend.

Also, you should never admit that you think your friend is fat. No good can ever come from this. Don't forget it's the little white lies that hold the fabric of our society together.

As with many of life's dilemmas, I say: look to the bard. It always pays to know your Shakespeare. That man explored every conflict you can imagine in a history, comedy, or tragedy, and if you update the slang a bit, the South is just loaded with plots from his plays. What I want you to remember from this analogy is what happened to all those messengers of doom and gloom. Were they ever gratefully and graciously thanked for imparting terrible news? No, they were not. They delivered their juicy news and exited the scene—after being run through with a sword, or after having their eyes gouged out, or after being banished from the kingdom. None of those fates makes for a happy ending for the messenger.

Ten Things Better Left in the Past

1) There is no reason in the world for you to publicize your pre-baby weight. No good can come from the unflattering, then-and-now comparison. I know a woman who refuses to weigh at all—even at the doctor's office. She just says no. I'm one of her great admirers.

2) The sordid details of your previous marriages. Spare us all, please. This information should be divulged on a need-to-know basis only.

3) Your natural hair color. All that matters is how cute your hair looks today. Too much factual information can be confusing if you've gone in a completely different hair-color direction.

4) Your prescription-medication history. Unless you have an unusual new disease fresh out of the rain forest that we might have read about in a magazine, or you have been attacked by an exotic animal, your medical-treatment regimen is not nearly as interesting to the rest of us as you might think.

5) Labor and delivery stories. They can't ALL be that bad. We're still having babies, aren't we?

6) Your high-school sports career. It is hard for me to believe that all of the forty-something-year-old men in my acquaintance who claim to have "played a little ball" in high school or college actually did. It's a statistical impossibility.

7) Your overcoming-addiction stories. We're proud of you for doing it; really, we are, but . . . enough already.

8) Your vacation photographs. We're glad you had fun on your vacation. We want to hear all about it, and the photographs make your itinerary come alive for us back home. However, one picture of you standing in the Roman Coliseum is enough. We don't need to view it column by column with you. We have art-history coffee-table books with professional photographs and inscriptions if we want to read them.

9) Your college fraternity and sorority sportswear. You're just too old. Accept it. You used to look precious in your sweatshirt with Greek letters. Now, you look slightly grotesque, like some kind of modern pop-art statement. Pack your sportswear away like the rest of us did, and save it for your children. If you don't embarrass them too much now, they might pledge the same fraternity or sorority that you did in a few years.

10) Family feuds. There should be a statute of limitations on sibling rivalry, petty inheritance battles, and which-kid-Mom-and-Dad-loved-best sagas. Nobody wins.

The Parade Only Goes in One Direction

Marking Time

I'VE NOTICED THAT EACH OF US MARKS THE PASSAGE of time differently, in personal ways that have nothing to do with calendars, impossible-to-calculate Roman numerals, or birthdays. Women, in particular, count the passing years in odd ways. For example, women often use their children's ages to date an event. A woman might say, "I know that reunion was April of 1984 because my son had that black eye his cousin gave him on Easter Sunday." We women sometimes use our own aging process as an hourglass for the past. I once settled a family argument by claiming, "I'm quite sure that trip was in 1997 because you can see right here in this photograph I'm wearing that size-eight winter coat, and I haven't seen single digits in years!"

I like to think of the way we women date the important happenings in our lives—before sagging ankles or after—as a colorful approach to the inevitable march of time. Occasionally, however, my mellow, aging-is-a-natural-process philosophy gets slapped by reality, and I suddenly notice the passage of time as if it is new—as if time has somehow picked up speed.

Once, when my children and I were reading a book about Koko, the signing gorilla, we stumbled upon a tricky question. Ever conscious of setting a good example, I said, "Let's look that up!" When I glanced around from the shelves where I was diligently searching for gorilla books, I saw that my children had automatically piled up in front of the computer.

My grandmother said she knew that times had changed when she called a neighbor to kill a snake in her yard, and he showed up with a golf club instead of a garden hoe. That was it for her—the symbolic end of her generation.

I'm beginning to understand how she felt.

Something My Mother Would Have Done

As an adult, have you ever done something out of character and thought, "I can't believe I am doing this. This is something my *mother* would have done"? I'm not talking about one of those kind, thoughtful things your mother did that everyone remembers her fondly for but, rather, one of those annoying, old-person things like wearing a raincoat to the ball game because there is a miniscule chance of rain.

I just had my first, full-fledged senior moment recently, and I'm not proud of it. I'm afraid that if I'm exhibiting this sort of behavior in my forties, my children are going to have to take me out back and shoot me like Old Yeller when real senility sets in.

It's kind of hard to confess this, so I'm just going to come right out and say it: I bought a sign for my front yard. That's right. You read that correctly. It's a small sign, very tasteful black iron, ridiculously expensive, and, I'm afraid, alarming evidence of the peculiarities we all develop as we age. I don't think I'd have bought the sign ten years ago.

The sign says: CURB YOUR DOG.

The wording of the sign was the subject of lively debate at my house. I was all for a "No Dogs, Please" sign. In my view, that phrasing was a polite request, a gentle reminder of the responsibilities of pet ownership. My husband thought the phrase was just plain confusing. "People aren't going to know what you're talking about," he claimed. "Are you afraid the dogs may bite you? Do you want to keep the dogs out of your azaleas? Are you just anti-dogs in general? Too vague about the dog-poop problem," he argued.

My children, who appreciate humor along the lines of booger jokes and classic selections of bathroom humor, lobbied for signs advising dog owners to "Scoop the Poop" and those picturing dogs squatting in mid-poop with the international circle with a red line slashing through it to show the property owner's disapproval.

How rude, crude, and unattractive, I thought. I was looking for something a little more tasteful. In addition, I had no desire to become known as the old lady who hates dogs. I *like* dogs. In fact, if we had a big enough yard, and I could envision a future when I would like to feed, water, and schedule health care for anything else—I already care for five humans, ten fish, and one eighteen-year-old cat that refuses to go into the light—I'd probably adopt a dog.

The point is that I do not have a dog. Unfortunately, you'd never know that to look at my yard. We live on a busy street. We have sidewalks and constant activity—runners, bikers, strollers, walkers, and dogs of every description.

It never ceases to amaze me that people take their dogs for walks, so they won't poop in their own yards, I assume, and then allow the dogs to poop in my yard without cleaning it up or suffering a pang of guilt. Since my children play in my yard every day, about three times a week I clean dog poop out of the tiny crevices in the bottoms of their athletic shoes using toothpicks, paper towels, and lots of disinfectant. This is not an activity designed to make me a happy camper.

Let me just say right here that of course I realize all God's creatures have to poop. I don't even mind if they poop in my yard as long as the creatures' owners clean it up. I'll graciously provide the paper towels and trash can, but I resent cleaning up dog poop when I DON'T EVEN OWN A DOG.

Because I am a reasonable woman, I am open to compromise. I'll grant dogs a free poop zone close to the sidewalk. The city owns an easement anyway. The poop is easy to spot and avoid on the edge of the lawn. But I'm fed up with dealing with a hysterical daughter who performs cartwheels straight through a dog-poop pile or a football-playing boy who's tackled right on top of a sneaky, early morning dog-walker deposit.

I realize I am bordering on the irrational here. Writing about dog poop is, quite frankly, a new low for me. I would much rather address more lofty topics, but I'm at the end of my tether on this subject. Sometimes I ask myself, is it really worth all this fuss? What's a little dog poop between neighbors, right? I guess it is just that rude, selfish behavior takes my breath away. I wouldn't dream of allowing one of my pets to cause some stranger to have to clean up poop, so it is hard for me to imagine that millions of ordinary, tax-paying, otherwise sane, rational citizens do that on a regular basis.

I've never quite had the nerve to yell at someone from my porch when I see his or her dog assuming the position for the inevitable, but I am quietly scandalized. I just can't bring myself to actually address a perfect stranger with regard to a pet's bodily functions. In fact, I'm uncomfortable with the euphemism "poop," but I can't think of a more palatable alternative.

It's enough to make me reach for the Tylenol.

So, I hotfooted it down to my local hardware store and ordered a hundred-dollar sign for my flowerbed. I picked it out of a catalog at the store rather sheepishly but felt vindicated when I saw the stack of signs waiting to be picked up—some of which were not nearly as polite as my own, I'll have you know.

I think maybe the sign will help, but my oldest son says it won't.

"You know what's going to happen to your sign, Mom?" he asked.

"What?"

"Somebody is going to steal it. You need to prepare yourself."

I was speechless at the thought. If that happens, it's all-out war. I'll build a fence around my front yard that'll make the White House lawn look accessible.

I'm not fooling around anymore.

Invisible Women

I REMEMBER THE FIRST TIME I READ RALPH ELLISON'S *Invisible Man*. I was in high school, and it made me look at south Alabama and the people around me in a different way. Growing up in the South, I heard discussions about race, religion, and politics as regularly as I heard bragging about the upcoming weekend's football game. Those discussions didn't seem to be the subject of great literature to me. They seemed like regular life.

When I was a child, these discussions sometimes became jumbled in my brain. I remember thinking God must be an Alabama football fan and worrying about whether or not there were two Santa Clauses—one for white people and one for black people—or just one. It didn't matter a bit to me as long as Santa could fit his fat fanny down my chimney every year.

Such debates were part of daily life, not something saved for highbrow intellectual debate on the television news. Everybody from the bank president to the bag boy at the Piggy Wiggly had an opinion on race relations, the

Alabama and Auburn football schedules, and which pillars of the community were and were not walking tall on the path of righteousness—who was cheating on whom.

As a child, I first observed that most Southerners have an inclination to share their opinions frequently, loudly, and with everyone who will listen. In the South, these debates are strung out, highly seasoned, beaten to death, overcooked, and served up in countless small dishes every day to everyone who is old enough to read the newspaper and vote. Some Southerners love to call in to talk-radio shows to rhetorically state, "If you ask me . . ." I'm telling you that it's a reality show down here.

I was born here, and I wouldn't call one of those radio shows if you held a gun to my head because I know better than to ask a Southerner for his or her opinion on politics, religion, football, or race relations unless I have all day to stand around listening to the answer. Southern men, especially, seem to have strong views on every subject, and they're always eager to share them with the rest of us to help us see the light.

After I grew up, I began to pay more attention to the nuances in Southern society. It took a couple of decades for me to notice that there is an invisible group of people in the South, an invisibility that has nothing to do with skin color.

In addition to the group of Southern women we all know—those who have no trouble whatsoever in expressing their bossy selves—there is a smaller group of women you don't hear from often. Of course, I realize they're not unique to the South; I'm sure they exist in every culture and society in the world. The common denominator for these women is they are virtually invisible to the rest of us scurrying by.

I'm talking about invisible women. They're everywhere. They come in all ages, colors, shapes, and income brackets. They live in every social demographic. They appear in every generation. They are born to every family. There's at least one in every circle of friends.

I'm here to emancipate the South's invisible women. They need a polite, toned-down, well-mannered version of the "we're here; we're queer; get used to it" battle cry. I've always agreed with the old saying that you catch more flies with honey than vinegar.

There's a reason that's an old saying, you know.

I feel sure that if the invisible women in the South went on a pound-cake or biscuit strike, they'd get the appreciation and attention they deserve pretty darn fast. I think they need to form a union. They should hire a lobbyist and apply for political asylum somewhere—maybe at a day spa. They could make a pretty convincing argument that they are an oppressed population.

We all know a few of them. They are the ordinary women who never stand out in a crowd but who weave the entire fabric of our society together. I think we have an unusually high number of invisible women in the South, and I've been worrying about that. I bet if you think about it, you can name a couple of invisible women in your own life, can't you? Think back on sisters, great-aunts, cousins, in-laws, friends from childhood. If you're like me, some names are bound to pop into your brain.

These women don't have obvious talents. They don't sing solos in the church choir, but they often make up the joyful noise from the church pews. Their voices are not particularly strong instruments, but if the choir director is out sick, you can hear the invisible woman's voice plowing along loyally with the priest's, keeping the hymn going strong until the last line.

They don't have stellar careers. No one wants to interview them. People rarely ask for their opinions on politics, religion, race, or anything else. They would be reluctant to voice them anyway. They are good listeners and are genuinely thrilled by the success of the women and men around them.

These women are not the most physically attractive among us. Their beauty shines from deep within, and you have to look hard to spot it. Their faces are often shiny as they cook for large groups. They know you can never tell who will drop by in the South. It pays to have homemade chicken salad, pimento cheese, and sweet tea ready for visitors. They know that every person who stops by for a visit in the South should be offered refreshments.

Invisible women are often not the most well-educated among us, although they usually help educate someone else along the way— children or a husband—and they are often well read because they never get over their childlike curiosity for all things new. They are always interested in hearing about what young people are reading, and they are able to discuss the *Harry Potter* series with the rest of the third graders because they took the time to read every word. More importantly, they enjoyed it.

They are usually the stay-at-home mothers. They are the women who push your child and their own in the swings at the park. They often make do with a little less materially in order to afford special treats for their children and yours. They never really bought into that whole quality-time-verses-quantity-time theory.

They are not powerful, and they never seem to be too busy to talk to those around them who are lonely. They take a few minutes in the grocery store to talk to the little old lady about the Jell-O recipe she is making for her grandson who is coming for a visit on Thursday. The invisible woman considers this time well spent. When she talks to you, whether you're the CEO of a huge corporation or the one girl in the senior class who didn't get an invitation to the party, she makes you feel like your conversation is the most important thing happening in the world at that second. Her eyes never stray from your face to see who else is in the room. She never interrupts a conversation with a real, live person to talk on the phone. If it's important, she reassures you, they'll call back.

These women are not wealthy. They rarely have prominent social standing, or if they do, it is of no importance to them. They don't work out at the gym, although they might ramble around the neighborhood in the afternoon looking for a few end-of-season blossoms to arrange. Their clothes are out of date, comfortable instead of stylish, serviceable rather than flattering.

They are rarely the chiefs of community, school, or church projects, but their names can always be found on the volunteer lists.

They are not the most interesting women we know. They are often quiet, a bit shy, late bloomers who are content to be observers to most events. You find them on the sidelines of the festivities. They are always present, forever the polite audience, eager to clap, to exclaim, and to praise the performers around them. They do not seem envious of the success of others.

Instead of being the belles of the ball, they can usually be found with aprons on over their cocktail dresses, refilling platters of party food, making sure everyone else has what they need. Their joy is in providing and observing the pleasure of others.

There is an invisible woman in every family, a woman who quietly washes dishes while everyone else sacks out in front of the television after a holiday feast, the one who remembers to wrap up the leftovers and a-little-something presents for all the senior citizens on her street who won't have anything to open on Christmas morning because all their friends and family are either dead, moved away, or housebound. This is the woman who shares the box of hand-dipped Swiss chocolates her nephew sent her for the holidays with the children of her gardener.

Every church has an invisible woman. She is the one who makes extra dishes for the potluck dinners because she knows that others often cannot or will not do their part. She is the woman who sweeps out the church and cleans up after Bible school is over when everyone else has gone home to recover. When she finds lost and abandoned Bible-school crafts under the pews, she carefully rescues them and puts them on tables in the parish hall so they can be reclaimed by small artists on Sunday.

Every school has an invisible woman. She helps with safety patrol when it is freezing and rainy outside. She chaperones the hot, sweaty field trips when no one else wants to drive, and she is the mom who the teacher trusts to transport the problem student. It is she who volunteers to pot twenty-five sunflowers so that each child can take home a Mother's Day surprise, yet no one talks about her work at the PTA meetings, and few people know her name.

The invisible woman is the small but vital cog that makes the machinery in the rest of our lives run smoothly. No one really sees or notices her work although everyone around her benefits from it. No one thanks her, and she would not wish to be thanked, especially. She works for others because that, truly, is her pleasure. She doesn't feel imposed upon. She isn't a martyr. She doesn't regale those around her with endless sighs and tales of woe and self-imposed suffering. She has a quick smile, a curious mind, and willing hands.

She is essential to our lives and yet overlooked. She is like water in America—nothing to be remarked upon, always there when you turn on the tap. She is like clean air, invisible and indispensable.

And then one day something happens to the invisible woman. She dies.

Her children organize her funeral. It is a modest affair, just what they think she would like. They pick fresh flowers from her garden for her coffin and arrange them together, just as she taught them to do, and they tell their priest that only a few pews will be needed for her funeral service.

"She didn't ever have a real job or join any social clubs," they say, almost apologetically.

The priest gives them a strange look, and then he smiles and says, "We'll see."

At the appointed hour, the church begins to fill, and fill, and then to overflow. There is no standing room left. Her children are amazed, confounded, as people from all walks of life come to tell of the small kindnesses their mother did to change others' lives, to help them through difficult circumstances, to do good for friends, acquaintances, and strangers in small ways that have been remembered for a lifetime.

"Did you know your mom bought me that navy blazer to wear to graduation? No? I never forgot it."

"Do you remember when your mom talked my dad into letting me go to summer camp? I can still see her face, talking to my daddy, making him think it was all his idea in the first place. She was something, your mom, wasn't she?"

"When my husband died, your mom came over every afternoon for two weeks and played with my children so I could go through all the insurance papers. It was the nicest thing anyone could have done for me then. I don't know how she knew I needed that time to plan what to do with my life."

Hours later, the invisible woman's children leave the church together, profoundly sad and heart-burstingly proud all at once. They can only say, "We never knew. We never imagined."

Conversations With Dead People

HAVE YOU EVER FOUND YOURSELF MAKING A MENTAL note to tell someone about something that happened to you, a trivial bit of news you know that person would relish; mentally saved up a choice morsel of gossip; or smiled in anticipation of the reaction you expect when you relate recent shenanigans only to realize, with a belated shock, that the person you are planning to tell is dead?

I hope I'm not the only person out there talking to myself AND dead people. I have, at times, questioned my own sanity and determined that although I can distinguish the living from the daisy pushers, my brain occasionally seems to willfully jump its track to continue sharing amusing anecdotes and all the other wonderfully ordinary events of daily life—never mind a little thing like mortality. I've asked myself the standard emergency-room-orientation questions, and I can name the current president and get close on the exact date, but somewhere, deep down, I still long for contact with all the people

I have ever loved, the living and the dead.

I can't decide if this is one of those comforting mind games our brains play to fill the void of missing people in our lives or if we continue in some way to commune with all those who have gone before us. All of this is just *way* out of my theological and meta-physical comfort zone. But I admit to feeling the presence of all those "others" sometimes, a comforting, you-are-not-alone feeling, as if it's okay to share a one-liner with a deceased friend because I already know what he or she would have quipped in response.

Maybe love is just so strong you can feel it from one world to the next. Love may, in fact, be the strongest force in the universe. It is, after all, one of the primary catalysts for human behavior, yet it is something intangible and impossible to prove. Strangely enough, most of us hard-core, show-me humans—those of us who struggle daily with issues of faith in our religions—still believe in love. If asked, most of us say we believe love exists. We are convinced of it, have seen evidence of the power of love in our lives: love between children and parents, lovers, and friends, even between humans and animals.

The last words from a dying person's lips are almost always words of love or caring, not expressions of hate or enmity. And love doesn't end with death, does it? The object of affection may be six feet under the ground, but the love and longing for that person do not end. Grief is, in fact, frustrated love.

Katharine Hepburn has a great line in the movie *Love Affair* about just this subject. In reply to a question about the wedding ring on her finger, she says, "Dearie, I am married—although my husband has been dead for years."

I know exactly what she means by that, don't you?

Things I am Too Old to Worry About Anymore

The bird flu. If I get it, I get it. I figure the CDC doesn't need any suggestions from me. I'll take my chances with the rest of suburbia. I refuse to freak out at the sight of every dead bird. Surely, some birds die of old age. Some get eaten by naughty cats or torched by electrical wires. Every dead bird is not fodder for a Stephen King movie.

Aliens from outer space. If they land in my front yard, I'll deal with them. I'll invite them in, call the mayor, serve them refreshments, and frighten them to death with a little daytime television. They'll be blasting off to a new galaxy before you know it.

The good china and the guest towels. Who in the world are we saving everything for? Do we think Queen Elizabeth might drop by, so we need to be ready with the Wedgwood? You know who washes the good china and the guest towels at my house? I do. I think I deserve to eat my frozen waffle on the antique Haviland. In the same vein, why should I dry my face with the same towels I send with my boys to summer camp? Don't I deserve a little monogramming, a little lace on my towel trim? I think I do.

The stock market. I don't own any stock, so what do I care?

Whether or not I have a VPL (visible panty line) on display. Newsflash: I wear panties. Every woman I know wears panties. I'm a proud full-brief-panty wearer in a world of thongs and low-riding pants.

Whether or not my daughter's hair is cute or not. It's an old, tired argument. Me: "Your hair would look adorable cut in a bob to frame your face. Let me have it cut just a few inches." My daughter:

"Short hair is for babies, Mom." Fine. I make sure her hair is clean. I buy ribbons for the ponytails. That's as far as I'm willing to go. That is not a battle I can win.

Being the oldest mother at my youngest child's college graduation. So I'm a little older than most of the other moms. My clothes aren't as cute. I have no idea who Justin Timberlake is. I don't care what music my children listen to on their iPods as long as I don't have to listen to it, too, and it's not completely tasteless. I prefer to look at the advantages to being an older mom. I've been around the parenting block a few times. I bet those young mamas don't know where the adults-only bathroom is hidden at the elementary school. You have to chaperone a dozen field trips, bake a hundred or so bake-sale cookies, and cut out hundreds of bulletin-board decorations before you get the key to that golden door. I always say there are advantages and disadvantages to every age.

Whether or not my children are flossing their teeth on a daily basis. I make the dentist and orthodontist appointments. I drive my children to them. I pay for them. I buy toothpaste, floss, and toothbrushes in endless supply, which vanish after every sleepover. I tell my children all the time, "You better take care of those teeth! The next set comes in a box." Truly, I've done all I can do. When they were little, I brushed their teeth for them. I'm not brushing the teeth of anyone taller than I am now. It's just a little rule I have.

Global Warming. I KNOW it's a big deal. I read. I get it. I recycle. I walk instead of drive when I can. I wear sunscreen, and I badger my kids to wear sunscreen. Lord knows I haul around tons of kids in carpools. I vote. I pay taxes. Although I hope my children do not discover this for a very long time, there is actually a limit to my powers. No matter what, I'm not giving up air conditioning. Period. That is not going to happen. I'm not into that kind of self-sacrifice. Global-warming guilt reminds me of a conversation my husband and I had when our second child was born. Standing in the doorway of the nursery, watching me change our baby's diaper with the quick hands of a professional card shark, my husband had the audacity to muse, aloud, "I wonder if we should use cloth diapers instead of disposable. Wouldn't that be better for the environment?" I gave him a look that made clear he'd crossed the line into hostile territory, and he'd better take a step back. "I'm not giving up disposable diapers," I told him. "Scientists will just have to think of something else." That was the end of that discussion. I'm afraid air conditioning and disposable diapers are deal breakers for me.

Organic Produce. I wash everything—fruits and vegetables—but I cannot spend another second of my life worrying about farmers and what products they are using to grow their vegetables. I figure they're eating what they grow, right? If it's good enough for them, it's good enough for me. After all, I've eaten cookies off the floor of my kitchen (I assume you are familiar with the five-second rule). I've finished half-eaten chicken fingers on my kids' plates for years. I firmly believe that's how these hips came to be the beauties they are today. I admit I am not as picky as some people. We don't have time for delicate orchids around this house.

SWAG
Communication

SWAG Talk

BEFORE YOU READ THIS, I WANT YOU TO CLOSE YOUR eyes, prop your feet up, and spend a minute or two thinking about the different conversational styles of your closest friends, the bosom buddies who make up your inner circle. I know it seems like a strange request, but keep reading, and I promise you an "aha!" moment shortly.

My friends have amazingly different—often polar opposite—conversational styles, and I'm beginning to think it's not a fluke. My theory is that we are all attracted to people who are similar to us in our core beliefs. However, in style—as opposed to the all-important substance of things—I've found that women are remarkably tolerant of each other's peculiarities and personality quirks when it comes to different ways of expressing themselves.

A small sampling of the smorgasbord of conversational styles would include: friends who talk too much (until your eyes glaze over), friends who talk too fast (at the same speed as

Japanese commuter trains), and friends who ramble on and on (until you consider feigning illness to escape).

When women speak of friends who have unusual hang-ups, we usually view these idiosyncrasies as a mere nuisance. I have noticed that men, on the other hand, see such superficial flaws as character defects and tend to steer clear of their oddball friends with all possible haste, as if the oddity might somehow be contagious.

I have a friend who doesn't like to ride in elevators. Boy, have I ever hiked some stairs for her! Do I see her elevator phobia as grounds for blacklisting her from my life? Certainly not! I spent a few years trying to coax or bribe her onto an elevator. Then, when I realized that only a much more qualified counselor than I could address her elevator issues, I offered to go with her to counseling sessions. When that didn't work, I agreed to take her out to lunch and get her sloshed every time she has an unavoidable elevator on her calendar. That's the way women work. If we can't solve a problem, we work around it. My elevator-challenged friend and I simply arrange our outings to avoid elevators whenever possible. We then moved on to juicier gossip.

Most men are unwilling to go to all that trouble. When a man discovers a bizarre personality hiccup in one of his friends, an elevator phobia, for example, he will argue logically and painstakingly with the friend, taking care to use computer graphics, color-coded diagrams, and safety statistics from elevator manufacturers to try and explain his friend's fear away. When this tactic fails, as it inevitably does, the man simply washes his hands of that friend, salving his guilty conscience with the knowledge that he tried to help.

No woman would do that. She'd simply pack her walking shoes when touring the Sears Tower with her friend and consider it part of God's plan to work off a few of the fat grams she and her friend consumed with lunch.

I have only recently become aware of how this tolerance applies to conversation. I'm willing to bet that all of you have at least one friend whose heart is as good as gold. This woman would not hesitate for a second to give you the control-top stockings right off her fat hips if you were in need of some tucking in after a run-in-the-stockings emergency. This woman, nevertheless, has never in all the years you have known her asked you a single question about the goings on in your life. To be fair, she really just doesn't have the time. She is way too busy updating you on the happenings in her life since she has last seen or talked to you.

When this woman breezes into your living room, you could be lying prostrate on the sofa with bloody teeth marks on your side forming the unmistakable shape of a shark's mouth, and she will not pause to inquire about the shark attack until she has told you every detail about the recent garden-club trials of her life. This woman always has a more tiresome husband, more difficult children, and a generally heavier burden to shoulder than you or anyone else you know, have ever known, or will ever know.

Another conversational category of friend we all have at least one example of in our lives is the passive-aggressive speaker. All of this woman's conversations are littered with sentences like: "Well, I *guess* we could do it that way, but I've never heard of anyone else doing that in the history of the world . . . That would be okay . . . if *you* really want to . . . although I never would have thought of doing it that way myself . . . but, of course, if that is all you can do. . . ."

Maddening.

Perhaps the most aggravating of all conversational styles is the shameless ignorer. This woman is tricky because she seems to be listening when you speak, and she actually asks questions, such as, "How was your trip?" After you've launched into an enthusiastic response, however, you find out with her next question, "Should we make cheese straws for that party?" that she hasn't heard a word you've said. You learn that this conversationalist is actually interested in your answer to her original question, but she expects your response time to be short and sweet because her interest in your life, while heartfelt, is not terribly *deep*.

If you're really lucky, you'll have at least one or two friends who are deeply committed to more than a yearly exchange of birthday and Christmas cards. They really do care about the goings-on in your life as much as their own, and they want to hear every detail about your argument with your husband and what the plumber said about the possibility of having unclogged pipes in your downstairs bathroom in the foreseeable future. This friend actually enjoys hearing you whine on the telephone about the four places you had to go before finding the space-alien paper plates required for your child's science project, and, best of all, you feel immensely happier for having told her. You save up things to tell this friend. It's immensely satisfying to hear her reactions, which are generally in perfect accord with your own views, of course, and you get the same satisfaction from telling your best friend every sordid detail of recent escapades as you did by tattling on your sibling as a kid.

These rare friends are such satisfying and nourishing conversationalists that we can be generous and appreciate the humor in our other friends' conversational styles. I can even enjoy taking the stairs with my elevator-challenged friend because the time just seems to fly by. She is a gifted conversationalist, and listening to her is well worth taking the stairs, which is a good thing since I'm usually so out of breath, I couldn't keep up my end of a two-way conversation anyway.

I have an aunt who is a true genius of chat. After I've talked to her on the telephone or visited with her in person, I feel warm inside, as if I'd savored a steaming mug of delicious hot chocolate and then discovered it's fat-free. In our conversations, we've talked, exchanged news, jumped in, interrupted each other, rambled up and down current events like a roller coaster, and addressed subjects that matter to both of us. We've tattled on all sorts of people and both felt much better for it. I've got news for some of you: this is what the rest of us who can't afford counseling do. We talk to our girlfriends. I'd put my best friends up there with the best psychiatric brains in the country. Their advice is pure gold. It's *following* their advice where I sometimes run into trouble. They frequently want me to do things I have no interest in doing at all.

When I think back on talks with the great conversationalists in my life, I always have fodder for further reflection. Good conversation is food for the soul—broadening ideas to think about, if not to adopt; affirmation that our friendships are deep and lasting; and an abiding knowledge that the closest friendships are worth all the careful tending and stair climbing necessary to keep them flourishing. I'm not sure there is a more satisfying feeling in the world than a good natter with a friend.

I am not a great conversationalist, but I long to be. I am overwhelmed by noisy conversations easily, and I'm not skilled at cocktail-party chitchat, but if you are my friend, and you have a real life problem, I'll sit in the swing with you and chew on that problem all afternoon. I aim to improve my conversational skills. I would be highly embarrassed to be one of those friends everybody avoids thanks to Caller ID.

Canned Remarks

Southern women like me take pride in our ability to remain polite and well mannered in the most provoking circumstances. Although I'm not as skilled at this as I'd like to be, I know some Southern women of a certain age and social experience who could, theoretically, be tossed stark naked into a room full of people, and any one of them could whisk a tablecloth from the nearest table, shape it quickly and artistically into a glamorous caftan, and, as a finishing touch, pin a gardenia from the table's center piece onto her shoulder within seconds—all while entertaining onlookers with a humorous story about how she came to *be* tossed naked into a room full of strangers.

Awkward social moments are an inevitable fact of life for all of us, but one of the best-kept secrets of well-prepared Southern women is the supply of canned remarks we keep on hand to fill the painful silences created by ignorant, insensitive, rude, or unbalanced family members, friends, acquaintances, or complete strangers. Sadly, there are people who like nothing better than creating a scene that will cause indigestion for everyone present.

As the years go by, I keep adding to my list of helpful remarks. Some of the expressions I've found most helpful are:

"Is this the closest exit?"

"Well, obviously, he has issues."

"Maybe she needs to increase her dosage a little."

"I think they're just high-spirited."

"What a wonderful idea. Why don't you handle that?"

"I never thought about it like that."

"I'm sure he/she meant well."

"Maybe she just needs a nap."

"Let's think of this as character building."

"What were you thinking?"

"I have nothing to add."

"Check with me first next time."

"Things are bound to get better."

"It's probably temporary."

"I'm sure she'll come around eventually."

"I would love to hear more about that next time."

"Well, at least he's enthusiastic."

"You just never know with her."

"I'm open to suggestions."

"She's been under a lot of stress."

"She never has been able to hold her liquor."

"Can I get anyone anything from the bar?"

"I don't think I heard you correctly."

"There has to be a better way."

"Please let me help you with that."

"Is there someone I can call for you?"

"That man never ceases to surprise me."

"I'm sure he was just kidding."

"You always look lovely/handsome to me."

"Have you lost your mind?"

Wrap it Up

YOU CAN TELL A LOT ABOUT A WOMAN BY OBSERVING how she goes about fairly mundane tasks. For example, if you know what to look for, you can map out the personality of a woman by watching how she wraps a present. Sure, you could pay thousands of dollars for a scientifically based personality profile, the kind of study large corporations and Internet dating services now require as part of their interview packages, but why bother? Wait until the next birthday rolls around, and watch what happens when the woman you love heads to her gift closet and reaches for her wrapping paper.

I have a whole cupboard under the stairs devoted to wrapping paper, ribbon, boxes, tissue paper, and other wrapping accoutrement. It's about the same size as the cupboard Harry Potter slept in during his first eleven years with the Dursleys. It's not a fancy keeping room you see in new houses these days. It's a hole under the stairs. I'm very proud of my wrapping cupboard. I spent years dragging scissors, tape, and wrapping paper from numerous, scattered drawers and closets where these items were stashed separately around my house before I found a permanent location to house gift-wrapping supplies.

Not a week goes by that I don't have to dive into that cupboard to find something in a hurry. About twice a year, I climb all the way in there on my hands and knees, clean it out, organize it properly, hang different colored tissue paper on separate hangers, and generally do things with gift-wrapping paraphernalia that would make Martha Stewart proud. After washing the dust bunnies out of my hair and spraying disinfectant on my scraped knees, I vow never to allow my wrapping supplies to get in such a sorry state again. I threaten my husband and children with all sorts of dire consequences if I find them rooting around in my cupboard. I have everything arranged to my complete satisfaction under there; it's a very satisfying chore.

Usually, I have a stockpile of sufficient wrapping supplies for every occasion from bar mitzvah to college graduation. I have: gift tags; monogrammed calling cards; bags and boxes of all shapes and sizes; tape in a heavy, I-mean-business, black dispenser; scissors that cut different borders (you need to get some of these if all you've ever seen are old-fashioned pinking shears); a hole puncher—the works. I have cardboard boxes with holes punched in the sides to thread curling ribbon through to keep it untangled and at the ready. I have spools attached to the wall to dispense colorful, curling ribbon. I tell you it looks like a craft magazine photo shoot could happen any minute in there.

Unfortunately, that picture-perfect neatness only lasts a few months, at most. Inevitably, I begin to open the cupboard door and hastily toss in a few bows that are too pretty to throw away. I can recycle them for future presents, I figure. Before I know it, the level of pristine neatness falls, and the colorful chaos of ribbon, paper, and tissue rises waist high and threatens to overflow the tiny confines of the cupboard. Pretty soon, the cupboard floor looks like Christmas morning—the detritus *after* a family has opened and exclaimed over all the Christmas loot. It looks festive, like something you'd love to be in the middle of, but it's no longer tidy. It's a glorious mess!

As you might guess, I also have a gift closet. I try to keep it stocked with treasures all year long, gifts I purchase as I happen upon them in shopping excursions. I hate to shop under the gun for a birthday, wedding, housewarming, or baby-shower present. When I have a shopping deadline, I always end up spending too much money or buying something generic, a present I could just as easily give my great-uncle or the boy who mows my lawn. I despise a one-size-fits-all present. I like each token to be special, unique, even one of a kind. That's a pretty high standard. Because I always have a budget (horrid, inconvenient, unimaginative things), I have to purchase wonderful gifts when I see them—even if I don't know who the future recipient will be at the time of the purchase.

I have to admit to you, although my intentions are always good in this area, the constant shopping has been known to result in a short-term strain on the family budget. I believe that if you find a bargain buy on a sterling-silver bud vase, you have to buy it on the spot and eat red beans and rice for a week. It'll be worth it in the long run. Besides, red beans and rice is nutritious and low fat as well as cheap—you can look it up. I like to take the long-term view and focus on what a blessing it will be when a wedding invitation arrives in the mail, and I have the perfect thing in my gift closet. To me, this is guilt-free shopping. Because I'm not shopping for myself, I'm not spending a dime more than I would have anyway. If you are a woman, I am confident this will seem logical to you. If you're a man, you may be a little shortsighted when the credit-card bill arrives. That's been known to happen around here, too.

On a brighter note, I've found this philosophy works especially well when I'm on vacation. It's fun to shop in a new city with unfamiliar and unique shops. As long as I'm making gift-closet purchases, I'm not spending any more money on vacation than I would have anywhere else. See how it works? You know I'm right. There's no use denying it. Christmas comes around like clockwork every year, you know.

Once a gift is purchased, the real fun begins. It's time to wrap it. This is where you need to pay attention. Like I said, you can figure out everything you need to know about a woman by watching her select a present and then wrap it.

First of all, the next time you receive a present, take a few minutes to really think about its wrapped appearance before you open it. Is the present eye-catching? Is it, in fact, a work of art on the outside, regardless of what's inside? In general, are all the presents you have ever received from this friend breathtaking? (If it's one bad wrap job, I don't think it should be held against her. We all have days when the kids are sick, and all we have left is purple dinosaur paper, orange curling ribbon, and leftover Wal-mart bags.)

On the other hand, is the present a three-pack of inexpensive guest soaps thrown into a drugstore bag and dropped off a week after your birthday with the receipt still in the bag? Think about that guest-soap-gift statement for a minute. It's surprising what you can learn through old-fashioned observation of details.

On one extreme, there is the woman who has no intention of ever wrapping a present herself. She leaves present wrapping to professionals. She thinks nothing of paying as much for custom wrapping as she does for the gift inside. This woman only buys gifts in shops that gift-wrap on the spot to suit her. She does not think it is unreasonable to ask that thirty-two items that cost a dollar each be individually wrapped in handmade wrapping paper, especially ordered from Florence, Italy. This is the same woman who will then spend hours picking out thirty-two different combinations of paper and ribbon for the sales clerk to use in the marathon-wrapping extravaganza. She thinks this is fun. Needless to say, this is not the gift-store owner's favorite customer. This woman thinks beautifully wrapped packages are important. She just has no intention of ever wrapping them *herself.* (Incidentally, I suspect that this is the same woman who has never cleaned her own potties.)

Another extreme wrapping personality is the harassed shopper woman. You've never received a properly wrapped present from this friend in your whole acquaintance. She is way too busy to bother with the pesky details. She never wraps anything and conveys the impression that you are darn lucky she took the time out of her busy schedule to buy a gift for you in the first place. Her present arrives in a plastic shopping bag with the handles tied in a knot. It is unwrapped, and she usually just slows down while driving by your house to toss it toward your front door like a newspaper. In

her eyes, it doesn't matter if it breaks; she has fulfilled her obliga-
tion merely by purchasing something vaguely appropriate for the
occasion. She doesn't care whether you like her present or not. You
are merely an entry on her to-do list that she hastens to scratch off.
Presentation and delivery are mere fluff to her.

Next on the evolutionary wrapping tree is the bag wrapper.
This woman doesn't make bows, use tape, or fold corners. She can
find a gift bag big enough to stuff a Corvette into if she has to—
anything to avoid real wrapping. She thinks wrapping paper is old-
fashioned. Why start with something on a roll when there are inexpensive bags of every shape, color, and size in every discount store
in America? Add the two conveniently located drawstring handles,
and you can't beat it, in her mind. This is a no-nonsense kind of
gal. She would not be embarrassed to deliver a stuffed-animal birthday offering in a Hefty garbage bag if it was a good fit. She loves
gift cards and gift certificates and is not above writing a check on
the spot to cover any forgotten gift emergencies. She looks at gift
giving as just another monthly bill. Needless to say, she doesn't have
a gift closet or a wrapping cupboard. She is not the least disturbed
about this either.

Most of us fall somewhere in between these extreme wrappers. We have some wrapping paper on hand with suitable thematic
choices for every occasion. We stock up when school fund-raisers
come around or during post-holiday sales, but we don't make gift-
wrapping into a pseudoreligious experience. Overall, we're self-
confident, emotionally secure adults. We're above all that obsessive
nonsense. We wrap appropriately, inexpensively, and attractively.
Our wrap jobs won't provoke a round of spontaneous applause, but
our offerings are nothing to be embarrassed about either. If we're
caught in a time crunch, we're okay with delivering a present with
wrapping paper and ribbon that do not perfectly coordinate. We
do, however, have minimum standards. For example, we have the
grace to be ashamed of bows that have clearly been chewed on by
the baby or the cat.

Quite often, I've found, the true nature of a wrapper is danger-
ously apparent with every present. Those of us who make our own
bows feel innately superior to those lesser mortals who buy bags of

prefabricated bows in discount quantity. We spend hours searching for fabric ribbon (never paper) in all widths, shades, and textures. We lovingly flip through December magazine pages, and we wish we could afford to make a silk organza bow for everyone on our Christmas lists. We dearly love to find additional trinkets to tie on such as flowers, ornaments, or cookies cutters that coordinate with our wrapping themes.

I would be remiss not to mention one class of wrappers, a group I like to call the super wrappers. You can instantly identify their packages from five yards away, and someone invariably says they are too pretty to open. That is, of course, *de rigueur*, and an entirely appropriate response to obsessive wrapping behavior. These women have a significant ego investment in their wrapping gestures, and woe unto you if you do not rave properly over their creations. Rest assured some raving and carrying on is expected.

Between the wrapping personality types are women who wrap inventively when they have time but recycle most of the time. No discarded bit of ribbon, string, bag, or tissue goes unsalvaged by this woman. She is the Green party's wrapping poster child. She's an environmentally friendly wrapper. If you are a natural saver, then rewrapping is for you. Re-wrappers are especially grateful to receive beautiful packages from super wrappers because they see future present-wrapping potential with each present they open. In their eyes, each eye-catching present is a two-for-one deal.

Thanks to a big wedding and the births of three children, I will never have to buy a box. In fact, I worry that I have insulated my home with fire hazards by stashing all types of flammable paper products in my wrapping cupboard. I hoard all sorts of wrapping treasures like a compulsive squirrel, and if you don't mind giving someone a retirement present wrapped in a box with a picture of Santa Claus on it, I can always help you out.

Just remember: the way a woman wraps—or doesn't wrap—a present tells you all you really need to know about her. This little test right here could be the deciding factor in whether or not you decide to marry someone. I'm telling you that present wrapping is a big personality clue about how a woman will conduct her affairs in other areas of her life. You know those cute packages wrapped in the comic pages of the newspaper? That woman is thrifty. If you're looking for a woman who can keep the family budget in line, a newspaper wrapper is the one for you.

If you are lucky enough to receive a package swathed in homemade wrapping paper with a child's hand print or artwork, then you better be plenty appreciative because that took some serious wrapping time and energy—and patience with small children. If you are in the market for a good nanny or a woman with some volunteer time on her hands, then a woman who has time to make homemade wrapping paper is a good place to look, I think.

Remember: when you open your next present, take the time to do a little wrapping analysis. You may be surprised by what you discover. It's amazing what you can learn when you pay attention. When writers ask me for advice, that's what I always tell them. In everything you write, in everything you do, and in every relationship and every endeavor: pay attention. I promise you, it'll pay off in spades.

Body Language

ALL THINKING BEINGS HAVE TO COMMUNICATE TO survive. We all do so in different ways, of course, according to our different animal physiology, needs, environments, and innate programming. We humans use much more than our voices and brains to communicate with each other. The most obvious proof of this premise is that spoken language is much different than written language. To avoid confusion and miscommunication, written language has to be much more precise than spoken words. When we communicate by speaking, we can supplement our words. We use body language (arms and legs gesturing wildly), body posture, vocal intonation, and facial expressions—anything handy to get our points across.

Even small children understand this premise. A three-year-old conveys a not-so-subtle personal evaluation by saying to a playmate, "You are a poo-poo head." This statement is clear, precise, and easy to understand. However, as any three-year-old can tell you, even the most effective name-calling can be rendered more effective by calling someone a poo-poo head in a loud, sing-song voice, with one's hands on one's hips.

Southern women do not feel constrained by mere words. Oh, no. We're adept at saying one thing and meaning another. Once you know the code, however, it's not that hard to translate. For example, if you ask a Southern woman if you can borrow her lipstick, she might say, "Well . . . certainly," in a scandalized voice, with her eyes stretched wide open in shock and her eyebrows raised up to her hairline. You can safely assume she means: "What is wrong with you? Lipstick is a personal item. Why don't you just ask to borrow my spare panties? I haven't shared a lipstick since I was a ten-year-old girl. Who knows where your lips have been? You can borrow my lipstick, sure, but I'm going to throw it straight into the trash can when you give it back. What nerve!"

I can tell what my best friend is thinking even if she's halfway across the room. If she's listening intently to someone, and her eyebrows are pushed together, and her lips are pursed as if she's been forced to drink that tinfoil-flavored dry sherry British people like, or she's just barely holding on to some words that are about to spill out of her lips against her better judgment, I know I better get over there and rescue her from whoever's causing her grief.

In the same vein, she says she knows I'm irritated even if she can only see my legs under the table. I admit I thought she was telling a tall one there. She says that if my legs are crossed, and I'm jiggling one foot constantly or tapping it repeatedly on the floor, she knows I'm irritated half to death, and it's only my good manners keeping me from reaching across the table and throttling somebody.

I've always said that good manners can go a long way toward preventing wars from ever breaking out. A heartfelt apology and a thoughtful gift can calm troubled waters—even on an international level of diplomacy. I see nothing wrong with the occasional purchase of affection, especially among nation-states. I read somewhere that countries don't have friends; they have interests. I know a lot of people who are like that. In a similar vein, I have a friend who says she knows her daughters-in-law are going to love her. When I asked how she could be so sure, she said she plans to buy their affection.

I think that just might work.

Did you know there are individuals who make a living reading body language to predict human behavior? Some of these professionals are paid to evaluate the body language of jurors in potentially big verdict trials. I sure hope we have some of those people working at the US State Department because somebody sure needs to get a handle on North Korea's Kim Jong-il and Iran's President Ahmadinejad. We could all use some clues as to what those two are thinking. Now that I think about it, though, maybe you can't read the body language of crazy people with any degree of accuracy. I just don't know, but I hope somebody much more qualified than I am is looking into it. I would consider that a good use of my tax dollars.

Everyone who knows me knows I need lots of arm action, jumping around, and face-making to get my points across when I'm talking. That's because I'm a Southern woman. To a certain extent, an individual's body language is dependent upon cultural expectations. In cultures the world over, most women love a little drama, as long as our hair doesn't get too messed up. It spices up the day and keeps the mind sharp. A spat of intellectual fencing never hurt anyone, in my opinion.

Unfortunately, our body language does not always translate well to other cultures. For example, I think a Japanese man might mistakenly think a Southern woman is unhinged, in fear for her life, or worry that she presents a clear and present danger to others in the room if he were to see her throw a full-scale hissy fit in response to the handiwork of her thoughtless teenager who tracked muddy cleat prints across her new Persian rug. Because I'm a Southern woman, and I'm a typical product of my culture, I think throwing a fit over an easily avoided carpet-mess cleanup is an appropriate and even temperate response. That's because I know a typical teenager caught in such a blatant cleanliness violation would probably mumble a perfunctory, "Sorry, Mom," without checking his stride on the way to the refrigerator. The Japanese man might have a coronary. The American teenager wouldn't even pause to take out his iPod earphones. The resulting hullabaloo would be a cultural misunderstanding. It could happen to anyone.

A raised eyebrow can convey an attitude of skepticism, displeasure, contempt, or disdain with the simple movement of one set of muscles. No words are necessary. A woman's languidly dropped shoulder and an outstretched arm could mean come hither to amorous swains, or it could mean nothing. You have to be careful in translating body language. She could be giving you the green light to approach and buy her a drink, or she could be reaching down to pick up a quarter.

Research into the ways animals communicate with each other is a fascinating field. I love primates. Maybe it's a narcissistic love affair in that primates are so closely related to us (and you know how interesting I think we are), but I feel a strong affinity with the animals in the primate house at the zoo. For years, my children and I have followed Dr. Patterson's work with the Gorilla Foundation, Koko the gorilla, and sign language. One of my favorite books I read to my children when they were little was *Koko and Her Kitten*. And let me just say that if you do not cry when Koko's kitten gets run over by a car, then you are one sorry excuse for a human being. It's a true story, you know.

One of my favorite zoo memories involves a primate encounter at the Birmingham Zoo between a chimpanzee and my oldest child. My son was about two-years-old at the time, still riding in a stroller, in between spurts of leaping out and running full-speed to the next animal exhibit. When we reached the chimpanzee enclosure, my son jumped out of his stroller, ran up to the glass wall separating us from the animals, and pressed his hands and face to the glass in awe. Immediately, one of the chimps jumped down from a rock and pressed her face and hands on the opposite side of the glass in a mirror image of my son's position. (I know she was female because we went to the zoo at least once a week back then. We knew the names of all the animals in the zoo; we were the first to see the new babies, and we applauded each new blade of grass that sprang up.)

My son had a small blanket in one hand, and, for reasons known only to a two-year-old, he put the blanket over his head. This initiated a game. The chimp ran to get a brown paper bag that she proceeded to put over her head in Simon-says copycat activity with my child. The game of peek-a-boo went on until I tore my child away, and the chimp shrieked with anger, ran to the edge of her exhibit, and stretched out her arm to entreat my son to return for more playtime. She screamed for him until she could no longer see him. I felt mean breaking up their play. It was a genuine moment of sheer joy in each other's company and an example of species-to-species communication. Chimpanzees remind me of three-year-olds. They play at about the same developmental level.

One of the most colorful—and I mean that literally and figuratively—ways a primate communicates with other members of its species is found in the world of baboons. They use facial expressions and sounds like we do, but they also use their colorful backsides. I'm not making this up. Don't you just love it? The more color you see, the more they've got to say, I guess. I think that would be an incredibly satisfying way to communicate. When someone irritates me, I could just whip around and show 'em my backside, along with a helpful color-chart key. That would really show them what's what. Wait a minute! Isn't that what the socially unacceptable, often slightly amusing, unseemly sport of mooning is? Maybe mooning is not merely rude behavior but a biological imperative that can be traced back to our common ancestors, our baboon cousins.

Well. That explains a lot, doesn't it? The next time someone calls you a baboon butt, I want you to take it as a compliment. You are colorful, expressive, and an excellent communicator.

Compliments and Insults

It is sometimes hard to tell whether you are being compliment-ed or insulted by someone in the South. For example, if someone says, "She's kind of special," that could be high praise, as in, "She is a unique, wonderful, extraordinary, and talented woman." On the other hand, "She's kind of special," could be a euphemistic clause for, "She's a nutcase, freak, or weirdo." It could even be a reference to mental incompetence. The next time someone says to you, rhe-torically, "Well, aren't you special?" it pays to think that all the way through. You might ask, "Do you mean special as in Special Olym-pics?" It wouldn't be the first time an insult came heavily disguised in a cocoon of cotton-candy words. Sweet words can be offered in dulcet tones with deadly intent. It's all a matter of interpretation. In these days of super-sensitive free speech, it's hard to get away with simple name-calling. "Special" is one of those adjectives that can go either way. Consider the context. Southern women, in particular, have some special phrases that require a geographic decoder ring to decipher. Some examples:

"You are so sweet to think of me."
Translation: Move on. I do not want to pursue this topic of con-versation, and I'm not taking questions.

"Well, I think it would look cute on you."
Translation: That dress is absolutely hideous, but you are good-looking enough to pull it off if you insist on wearing it.

"Don't give it another thought."
Translation: You obviously forgot to give some subject the appropri-ate thought when it might have made a difference. Now, it's too late.

"Well, I just don't know what else you could have done."
Translation: If I'd found your husband with that woman, I'd have hit him over the head with a golf club, too. It was a completely understandable loss of temper.

"These things happen."
Translation: I'm so sorry your daughter fell off the stage into the orchestra pit during her ballet recital. I know she was embarrassed half to death, but there's just not a thing we can do about it, and we have worn this subject out.

"I don't think anyone noticed."
Translation: I don't think anyone noticed that your skirt was tucked into your panties when you came out of the bathroom. The ballroom wasn't all that crowded by then. It was just bad luck that you had to go up front to the podium to get that award.

"I'm sure you did your best."
Translation: It's a shame that your best is so woefully inadequate.

"I say we make the best of it."
Translation: They're married. We might as well be nice about it.

"It could have been worse."
Translation: He could have a criminal record, too. It's certainly not for lack of trying on his part.

"Well, at least it's different."
Translation: It's ugly as sin, but nobody else will be wearing it. That's for sure.

The Unexpected

The Accident

NOT LONG AGO, MY CAR WAS TOTALED IN AN ACCIDENT. Overall, I'd say it wasn't a great day, but it did have a couple of highlights that could only happen in the South. I'm going to focus on those since I can't do a darn thing about the rest.

Here's the story: I was in a turning lane, on the way home from picking up one of my children from yet another baseball practice. When my arrow turned green, I turned left, just as I've done a million times before, when a car suddenly zoomed into the side of my car like the T-Rex in Steven Spielberg's movie, *Jurassic Park*. That car just got bigger and bigger until it crashed right into us. I'm here to tell you, until I got my children out of our car and checked every inch of their little bodies for injuries, not one amusing thing happened. After I was sure we'd all live to fight another day, however, I had a double espresso high of relief going, and things began to look up. There is nothing like a good scare to jerk my priorities in line, and, frankly, there are few things I care less about than my car.

The very best thing about that accident is that the car that crashed into us was driven by a SWAG. I could tell the minute I met her that we were two of a kind, and I mean that in a good way. She climbed out of her car and was worried sick that everyone in our car was okay. She accepted full responsibility for the accident, apologized profusely, hugged me with one arm, and waved her insurance card with the other arm. Now, that may not be the insurance company's textbook idea for how to respond in the event of an accident, but for me, that was absolutely perfect—the best mannered response in the world. Those were the exact words I wanted to hear when, eventually, I was able to climb out of the passenger side of my car with two of my children in tow.

I have to tell you that the woman who crashed her car into mine is just the most precious thing. I liked her immediately, and I knew within the first five minutes we could be friends. I suspect this is one of those incidents that could only happen to Southern women in quite this way. After comforting my children by pretending accidents are an everyday occurrence (this was my first one) and securing their safety on a busy thoroughfare by seating them on a wall on adjacent property and putting the fear of God in them if they moved without my permission, I was free to go and comfort the sweet driver who ran her red light. It was starting to rain, and I whipped out my hot-pink umbrella and opened it over both of our heads as we hugged each other. I couldn't help it. She was desperately in need of comfort, and I was the only person available.

When the police officer arrived, he seemed a little surprised to find us happily sharing an umbrella and commiserating. We told our story together, politely, without a single exaggeration, a breath of defensiveness, or a hint of ill will. Two witnesses confirmed our polite version of the facts.

"Officer, it was all my fault," the other driver said, "those witnesses over there agreed that she had a green arrow. I don't even remember what my signal was! This is just so upsetting! I'm just so sorry!"

"Accidents happen, honey," I comforted her; "you didn't mean to do it. Everyone makes mistakes. I'm sorry about your pretty car, too."

She was driving a sporty new Lexus. It was a much nicer car than mine. Contact with my mama tank had not been pretty.

"It was a birthday present from my husband," she said. "He is not going to be happy. I just called him. He'll be here in a second."

I watched a shiny new Mercedes pull off the road about fifty yards up and said, "Is that him?"

"Yep," she said. "Does he look mad to you?"

"I'll stand here with you and help you explain it to him," I told her.

I firmly believe Southern women have to stand together, especially in emergency situations. A potentially angry husband is right up there on the top of my emergency situation list.

Just then the tow truck arrived, and we argued politely over who should have her car loaded first. "You go first, honey," she said, "It's my fault you're in this mess."

"No, you go," I said, "that little sports car of yours isn't going to take up nearly as much room as my big ol' car. Your vehicle looks pretty pitiful."

The tow-truck driver said he'd decide himself which car needed to be loaded first. We gathered he did not need our expert advice.

First, we waded through the debris together to unload birthday presents from her smashed car. (She was on her way to her grandchild's two-year-old birthday party. This tidbit, naturally, led us off into all sorts of offspring discussions.) She and her husband offered to take my children and me home, which I thought was just the sweetest thing. However, we'd already received about twenty offers of assistance from passing motorists who knew us personally, and I'd already bundled my children into a friend's car. (In fact, I managed to organize a ride for my son to his baseball game, I retrieved his batting bag, and I talked him out of hyperventilating—all in a timely manner so he wasn't even late for his game. I think that is pretty impressive parenting from the side of a busy thoroughfare when I felt like throwing up.) The other driver had to field her share of helpful offers from rubbernecking friends, too.

My new friend said she thought we must have picked the most embarrassing corner in the city to have an accident because every friend or acquaintance we'd ever known in the last twenty years seemed to have driven by in the last half hour. We certainly weren't going to be able to keep this little accident a secret. I thanked my lucky stars that I'd deigned to put on a bra before picking up my son from batting practice. I don't always do that when I'm just dropping off or picking up, and it would have been even worse to be sprawled on my back like road kill without my bra.

My sweet new friend, on the other hand, had on the most attractive new pair of shoes, a style I'd seriously considered purchasing for myself the week before until I remembered some expensive new orthodontist work I was facing with one of my children, and I reconsidered that luxury purchase. I complimented her on her shoe selection, and we enjoyed the shoe conversation for a few minutes. I was doubly reassured when I realized that a woman who paid that much money for shoes probably kept her insurance premiums up to date. It was just another good sign.

I warned her that she would probably end up in a book. I can't help that kind of thing. It's an occupational hazard. My life isn't really that interesting. I have to use all the material I can get. I was already composing sentences in my head, right there on the side of the road. This was just too good not to write about. As you might expect from such a sweetie pie, she immediately promised to buy a copy of the book. I think she was making a sorry-for-crashing-into-your-car gesture. I was touched. While I don't recommend a car accident to anyone, of course, I'll have to say that it was almost worth it to meet that woman.

Unfortunately, however, on the way home the light began to dawn on us. We now had to replace our paid-for, nine-year-old, six-rear-seat SUV, and I was shocked to learn it was worth virtually nothing.

My husband works an hour away from our home. We were in the middle of post-season baseball tournament play, and my boys were spread out in ballparks all over the city. The cold, hard reality was that we had exactly four days to find a new car. Then my husband would have to head out of town, and I would be stranded at home with three children out of school for the summer like a woman under permanent house arrest. Baseball tournaments stop for no one, and my boys' teams were separated by several suburbs and the continental divide, so one car was not going to cut it for long. The insurance company had graciously allowed us the use of a rental car for the weekend, so we were car shopping under the gun. Trust me: this is not how you want to buy a car.

My husband, innocent that he is, told the kids, "Of course, you can come with us to look at cars. It'll be fun!" As the seasoned, stay-at-home mom, I knew that was a mistake of monumental proportion.

"You three listen to me," I told them. "If you come with us to the car dealerships, you cannot talk to us the entire time we are there. We have to concentrate; do you understand? If we don't, there is no telling what kind of lemon we are going to come home with."

That statement provoked immediate interest in my youngest child. "They sell lemons at the car place?" she wanted to know.

"No, no," I responded, "That's just an expression."

My oldest child went straight to the shiny sports cars on the lot like he had magnets in his sneakers. "Mom! Dad! This is IT! This one is perfect! Come look!"

I took one look over my shoulder without breaking stride on my way to the wagon section, just to be polite, and asked him, "Son, how many seats do you see in that car?"

"Um, two," he said. It was easy for him to discern that information since his face was pressed against the driver's side window, and he was drooling with envy down the glass, lost in a daydream where he was seated in the driver's seat of a miniscule BMW convertible.

"And how many people do we have in our family?"

"Five, but we could take turns, Mom! This is a great car! You need to come and see it!"

"Check the sticker, honey. How much does that car list for?" I asked my son, the budding car salesman.

"Fifty-eight thousand and change, Mom. Is that a lot?" he wanted to know.

"Not for Bill Gates, sweetie. Let me put it this way: that's tuition at a private college. You need to be looking at cars with stickers that scream commuter college; understand?"

Meanwhile, I'd missed the entire explanation the salesman was offering my husband about a car that was remotely related to our needs, and my middle child was pulling me by the arm to look at a vehicle that was clearly designed for off-road use or desert warfare on the African continent.

"I like this one, Mom; what do you think?"

"Check the gas mileage, honey," I said, trying to make this little car-buying adventure into a summer-enrichment field trip, "What does it say?"

"It says 'twelve highway, ten city'; what does that mean, Mom?"

"It means that car gets the same gas mileage as a bulldozer, son. I'm pretty sure that it isn't the right car for us," I replied.

My seven-year-old daughter, incensed at being left out of the car purchase discussion, interrupted theatrically to say, "*Well*. If anybody in this family even cares what I think, I know what kind of car we should get, and it has room for our whole entire family, *and* it has a television and soft drinks."

For once, my youngest child had her older brothers' complete, undivided attention. The prospect of watching ESPN in the backseat had temporarily bewitched their minds.

"What kind?" they asked her in unison.

"We should get a limo!" she declared, triumphant, as if she had privately worked out a new trade route to China.

The boys agreed instantly, declaring it a perfect solution for all concerned, and all three children turned to their parents to see how we were going to react and possibly mess this up for them.

"You are bright children," I told them. "Can you identify the problems with that scenario?"

"Well . . ." my oldest son admitted, "there might be a problem with the driver. Do they come with the limo, or do you have to pay extra for them?" he asked the salesman suspiciously.

Before the salesman could unscramble his brains long enough to come up with an intelligent and yet sensitive response, my middle child interrupted with his own objection: "You can't buy people!" he declared dramatically. "Don't you even know about the 'Mancipation Proclamation? That's slavery! It's wrong!" said mister just-finished-Alabama-history-course boy.

"Don't worry, honey," I comforted him, "there is absolutely no possibility that we are going to buy a limo, and the driver doesn't come standard."

Although my children climbed into every car on the lot, poked and prodded every feature and option, peeked into every trunk, and climbed into every cargo area, we could not find a suitable car that afternoon, and our children were outraged. When we loaded them back into the rental car, they were astounded that their parents had been unable to choose a car on the spot and felt the day had been wasted if we weren't even going to take a new car home with us.

"I don't get it, Mom," my middle son said. "You get mad if we can't pick out a new cereal in about six seconds, but you couldn't pick out a car on that whole lot. There were tons of choices! That was just a waste of time! I could have been at the swimming pool."

"You're right, son," I said, "You three had some good suggestions, but I guess it just wasn't meant to be today."

Our three children exchanged baffled looks amongst themselves, and one son said, with an injured air, "We certainly did everything we could to help. You guys are on your own now."

Ten Ways Women are Ambushed by the Unexpected

Hair-color selection. Newsflash: the color on the box does not always match the color your hair will actually turn out to be after you color it. Hair coloring is always a little adventure. By the way, you won't look like the woman on the box either—just in case you were hoping for that little metamorphosis.

On-call physicians. Although we all believe our personal physicians are entitled to time off to have fun with the rest of us, it is decidedly disconcerting to greet someone you dated in college, standing in for your beloved obstetrician for the weekend, while you are wearing a paper dress, and he is seated on a stool between your knees.

Lapses in personal hygiene. It is always puzzling to me to stand downwind of someone with body-odor issues. If I can smell that person's dire need of soap, then surely he can smell himself, right? How self-absorbed do you have to be not to know you reek?

Children's questions. Children are curious. This is, of course, how they learn things they really need to know. Unfortunately, children do not discriminate with regard to the timing or appropriateness of their questions. It is easy to be caught unawares with a question such as, "Are you just fat, or is there a baby in your tummy?" or, "Where did you lose your arm? Do you want me to help you look for it?"

Unexplained noises from your bedroom. If you hear noises from your bedroom when you pop in unexpectedly for lunch, it is best to treat yourself to lunch in the closest restaurant with a bar. No good will come of opening that bedroom door to investigate. Think of it like a horror movie. Why in the world do people persist in checking out scary noises from the basement or attic? Get out of the house!

Crazy-person behavior. Resist the urge to ask crazy people to explain their actions. Do not try to reason or argue with a crazy person. It won't do a bit of good. Accept that whatever they claim to see or hear is real enough to result in your accidental-shooting death. They'll get inpatient counseling. You'll get a two-paragraph obituary. Move on.

Unexpected gifts. Do not assume there is a sneaky ulterior motive for an unexpected gift. Is it really so hard to believe you could have a secret admirer? Occasionally, nice things happen to good people, you know.

Old flames. Occasionally, in a world of four billion people, you will run into an ex-something-or-other who you could have happily lived the rest of your life without seeing again. If you are a Southerner, this is just bound to happen. Be gracious about it. Rise above any wish-you'd-said taunts regarding ancient relationship history. Acknowledge the maggot's existence and exchange a few seconds of meaningless small talk. Demonstrate that living well without him or her has been your greatest reward.

Pricing. Antique-store owners, in particular, sometimes assign ridiculously inflated prices to their wares—just hoping for an unsophisticated shopper with more money than sense. When you see a Southern woman whip out her reading glasses to scrutinize the zeroes on a price tag, and then you see her howl with laughter until coffee comes out of her nose, well, you're probably seeing a woman who knows her sideboards.

Weight gain. It's the scales. Those things are off all the time—not just in the South but all over the country—especially the week after Valentine's Day. Also, in case you haven't heard, jeans are being cut smaller all over the world. It's not you. You are the same size six you've always been. The jeans are just cut SMALLER than they used to be, especially through the hips and waist.

The List Lady

LIKE EVERY OTHER SOUTHERN WOMAN I KNOW, I like to plan for every contingency. It continues to amaze me that there are people in the world who never plan anything and seem to enjoy flying by the seat of their pants. It is possible, I admit, that they are a teeny-tiny bit more spontaneous and fun than I am. Of course, these are the same people—often perfect strangers—who borrow Band-Aids from me at the park because I have sense enough to pack a first-aid kit, needle and thread, bottled water, painkillers, chocolate, and an interesting book to read, just in case.

It is, therefore, hard for me to switch from plan A to plan B, C, or D, and even when I'm left with no other choice, I'm never too happy about it. To be completely honest, this list-making trait is not easy for every person I encounter to appreciate. It is not often a trait that endears me to others.

I've found it takes one save-the-day incident to convert the disparaging masses into believers. Send a hurricane my way, and I've got enough batteries to light up a football stadium; enough kerosene lamps to make this place look like something off *Little House on the Prairie*; a fireproof, waterproof lockbox with emergency cash and telephone numbers; a two week supply of medicines; power conversion cords for the car battery; and yards and yards of plastic sheeting to wrap my house up like a cocoon. (I'm not really sure what the plastic sheeting is for, but I've got it.) You should see who wants to be friends with the list lady when the power goes out for a few days.

I realize that the perfect plan isn't always attainable in real life, but I can't resist the urge to *try* to design and implement a plan for every scenario—with strategic options built in that would appeal to the Department of Homeland Security for an armed defense of our state's port city of Mobile, Alabama. We don't have firearms in our house, but my kids can secure the perimeter with a small arsenal of water pistols we keep in the pool bag.

I'm a mother of three children, so I've learned to live by the motto, "Give it your best shot." I can prioritize on the fly in a matter of seconds, and I can triage while running full speed to my car with one kid on my back and one under each arm. If I run into any of your kids along the way, rest assured that I will scoop them up, too, and keep them safe until the crisis is over. Moms know how to stick together in emergencies.

I have great difficulty with the religious admonition to turn everything over to God. Every time I try to do that, I find I need to remind God of a few more details he might have forgotten (seeing how he's been around forever and all that).

I like lists. I think they are delightful and pleasing in their simplicity. Lists give me an illusion of control even when it is blatantly obvious to everyone there is none to be had in the situation. Even if the list says something as inherently provocative as: (1) decide on burial or cremation, (2) pick out casket, and (3) check insurance policy for criminal exclusions, I find that list comforting. Lists make me happy in a way I find slightly disturbing yet oddly satisfying.

There's nothing like seeing your choices in black and white to help you sort the wheat from the chaff. If you take a CPR class, you will be taught a version of the ABCs that is different from the song you learned in kindergarten. The ABCs is really just the Red Cross's fancy name for a list. When you encounter an unconscious person, you are taught to shout, "Are you okay?" If you don't get a reassuring response, you check the victim's airway, breathing, and circulation. Then, if it has been a while since you took the CPR class, you try to remember how many breaths and chest compressions work for children and adults, depending on your current needs. If you have good sense, you'll ask someone to dial 911 and call in the cavalry while you're trying to remember your CPR class specifics. Luckily, when the young, well-trained paramedic arrives, she won't have to wipe red lipstick off her mouth with the hem of her dress before beginning mouth-to-mouth resuscitation. She'll have worked out all those kinks ahead of time.

I think it would be a good idea if we could all agree on an etiquette book filled with lists for handling ticklish social interactions, as well as emergencies. We could deliver it to each house like the telephone directory, and I think we would prevent a whole world of miscommunication, misunderstandings, and maybe even some armed conflict. The list should include:

1) Lists citing criteria used to decide who needs to be sued and who needs to be taken behind the barn to have the snot beaten out of them. This plan would save individuals and the state a heck of a lot of time and money. Just think how we could reduce the cases of judicial backlog! In addition, I think you'd get about the same percentage of satisfied litigants as you get with the traditional tortuous route to dispute resolution. A sincere apology and a sound thrashing would go a long way to settling most legal disputes.

2) We also need to agree on a list of basic social skills mastery that should be required for all those who wish to mingle in polite society. If you have not mastered a few rudimentary, entry-level developmental milestones, then you can't come out and play with the rest of us. For example, these seven little rules right here would make restaurant dining a much better experience for all of us:

    a) Refrain from scratching body parts.

    b) Avoid any nose picking.

    c) Wait to floss your teeth or blow your nose until you are in the restroom or—even better—back in the privacy of your own home.

    d) Chew with your mouth closed.

    e) Participate in small talk with your server (i.e. nothing along the lines of, "Yo, we're ready to order!").

f) Recognize the cleverly disguised fan napkin on your table for what it is and demonstrate the will to use it.

g) Be able to figure out an appropriate tip for your server without a calculator.

3) We also need to agree on a list of vacation rules and attach them to the back of every hotel door, right next to the fire-exit plan and the check-out instructions:

a) When sharing a public beach, please remember to cover all body parts routinely characterized in our culture as private territory, especially if the exposure of any part of your anatomy will provoke lascivious behavior from your vacation companion, which leads us to the second item on the list.

b) If you are suddenly moved to passion by the swanky resort wear of your companion—or the lack of it— please retire to your room to indulge yourself. Those of us who share beach real estate with you have no desire to observe your indiscretions, especially if we have no prospects of indulging in any indiscretions of our own.

c) Do not assume that any of the other resort guests in your vicinity share your taste in music (why bring a jam box to drown out the universally appealing white noise of waves, sea gulls, and lapping water?), secondhand smoke, or heated discussions with your spouse, children, in-laws, or friends.

d) Keep your sandy, sweaty bottom to yourself. Shower off before bellying up to the poolside bar or lowering yourself into a hot tub or pool. A vacation is no excuse for poor personal hygiene.

These lists could go on forever. I'm not even warmed up yet. I urge every one of you out there to come up with a list or two of your own. Think of it as your civic duty. One day, in a galaxy far, far away, we'll write that book together. A future beauty contestant (a.k.a. a scholarship winner) will say that world peace was eventually a reality, and it was all because of well-organized Southern women who came up with a book of lists—a simple, yet profound, solution to an ancient conundrum.

Have You Lost Your Mind?

On rare occasions, even Southern women are flabbergasted by an unexpected turn of events and find it impossible to immediately think of an appropriate polite response. If it is obvious that severe consternation is called for, you may hear a Southern woman utter the following words: "Have you lost your mind?" This is shorthand for, "I'm so appalled that I don't know what to say." This code is immediately and universally understood by husbands, children, and close friends all across the South.

Allow me to give you an example. I once used this expression myself when I walked out on my side porch and saw a couple of small boys throwing water balloons into my ceiling fan. "Have you lost your mind?" popped right out of my mouth. The expression could have been created for just such an emergency. It is true that I have never, in fact, actually said to my children, "By the way, don't ever throw water balloons at the ceiling fan." It never occurred to me that I could be genetically related to a group of imbeciles who would not know this instinctively, on a gut level, without being told. Of course, these are the same people who throw wet towels down on the carpet under the false impression that some good fairy—Mom—is going to hang them up, so I can't say I'm totally surprised.

The following list includes my favorite "Have you lost your mind?" scenarios. If you hear someone express the following sentiments, you can safely assume that disaster on an epic scale is about to erupt. My advice to you is: Run away! Quickly! Trust me. No good can possibly come from the drama that is about to unfold. Consider yourself forewarned. I've done all I can do for you. The rest is up to you.

The following phrases are classic precursors to ruin:

"Maybe just this once."

"I doubt it's loaded."

"How do you know they're real?"

"Maybe we should just take him/her home with us for a while."

"We've got plenty of time to evacuate."

"You're going to do *what* with your philosophy major?"

"As long as nothing else breaks, I think we can make it."

"I'd rather be trapped in the car with a rattlesnake than that child."

"Everything about this makes me tired."

"Well, it used to be bad manners. Now I think it's some kind of free-speech statement."

"I don't think you can have visitors when you're under house arrest."

"Well, I've never heard of a real-life case of amnesia in my life."

"That sound? It's probably just firecrackers."

"Are you trying to make me mad, or is this just your pleasing personality?"

"Do you have any actual proof that we're related?"

"My mother told me not to marry you."

"I always thought he'd end up in prison."

"I don't see how it could make it any worse."

"I've been dying to say this for years."

"Well, somebody better handle it."

"That check is probably still good."

"What do you mean *if* your divorce is final by then?"

"I don't think anybody has been killed doing this in years."

"I'm pretty sure the leak is fixed."

"I used to be able to squeeze in between these."

"What do you say we call this a do-over?"

"Did it grow like that?"

"It looks strong enough to hold both of us."

"Should we see if anybody's down there?"

"I don't need a life jacket."

"Do you think it's poisonous?"

"There's not a jury in the world that would convict you for that."

"This is not an area in which I am open to experimentation."

"Well . . . this is certainly a surprise."

SWAG Lists

MUCH TO MY SATISFACTION, I HAVE DISCOVERED that I am not the only Southern woman out there with an affinity for list making. Apparently, it's a habit that springs from the soul of Southern women as easily as dandelions in the springtime. Since I've been a compulsive list maker for as long as I can remember, I thoroughly enjoyed finding out that other women do it, too. The following is a list about lists. Get it? Here are ten things Southern women make lists about:

1) Very important instructions for our loved ones to carry out in the event of our demise. You'd think our bossiness would end with the grave—wouldn't you? No way. Southern women will not allow a little thing like earthly mortality limit their sphere of influence.

2) Lists of things those who love us need to do immediately, for example: clean out the garage, change the beneficiary in a last will and testament, or wash the car. Usually, a Southern woman adds a dash of guilt to speed things

along. She may say she hopes her loved one can perform this small service for her before she expires. Her death, she implies, could come at any second.

3) Daily errand lists, ad nauseam. I actually jotted down a list once that said: (a) make Chex mix, (b) pick up dry cleaning, (c) meet with detectives. I'm not making this up. The sad part is that this list is actually ranked in order of importance. While I was extremely interested in what the police detectives had to say about death threats, the Chex mix was for the school bake sale. When moms organizing the bake sale say, "Drop off baked goods at 8 AM," they're not kidding around.

4) Ongoing lists for redecorating. This list never ends. Just when you think a room is finished, something gets broken, wears out, or gets ruined by a small child or a seemingly domesticated small animal. Every woman I know has an envelope in her purse with swatches of fabric and measurements. You never know when you're going to happen upon a good garage sale or a decorator's showroom clearance sale. It pays to be prepared at all times to snag a bargain.

5) Christmas lists. It may be July, but if you see something that would be perfect for your mother-in-law for Christmas in the window of a store, you better buy it—even if you're on your way to the emergency room. The perfect mother-in-law present is like the sighting of an assumed-to-be-extinct bird. It's mighty rare. A few stitches in the chin can wait thirty minutes. It may hurt a little at the time, but it'll be worth it in December when you pull out the perfect present you've had tucked away in your gift closet for five months. Anyway, the chin stitches are either going to leave a scar or not leave a scar. A few minutes here or there won't make a bit of difference.

6) Telephone numbers. My experience has shown me that you never know when a game is going to go into overtime, a tire is going to blow, a child is going to throw up, or your best friend is going to have a marital crisis that requires your immediate presence. It pays to have a backup plan. We're talking cell-phone numbers.

7) Mental list of grievances. Of course, we don't write this list down on paper. We have more sense than that. But you better

believe that we're keeping a mental tally of grievances, both small and large, against those who have wounded us and those we love. Forgiveness is easy. It's forgetting that's hard.

8) Hospitality. Of course, we keep count. We know when we owe dinner parties, drinks, food offerings, baby-sitting, carpooling, and other favors to our friends. We'll repay everybody eventually. We'll get right on it as soon as the dining room is painted, the children leave for college, the bathroom mold is banished once and for all, and the grocery budget shows some flexibility.

9) Lists of household jobs. Even if she doesn't keep a list on the refrigerator, rest assured that every woman can tell you, off the top of her head, the list of things that need to be done around the house, in the yard, for work, for school, for church, and to properly address her own hair-coloring and dry-skin crises.

10) Wish list. Even if she never has an invitation or the opportunity to voice it, every woman has a wish list of places she'd like to go someday, activities she'd like to try, books she'd like to read, topics she'd like to discuss, and friends she'd like to visit more often.

You know what I think we should do? I think we should take the to-do list and replace it with the wish list. That would shake things up, wouldn't it? I think it would probably precipitate household mutinies all across the South. I can hear the imaginary screams, full-throated wails, and relentless whining that would spew forth from the mouths of children, spouses, teachers, coaches, clergy members, and other people accustomed to receiving the benefits of countless hours of to-do-list work from women all over.

I get a little giggle just thinking about pulling off a full-fledged strike. When you think about it, you realize there are all kinds of lists in the world. It's the priority of those lists and where one falls in the order of things that really tells the tale, isn't it? Choices, choices, choices. There's a whole roulette wheel of choices out there. I may just try something *a la carte*, something not even on the menu. There's no telling what could happen.

Mind Your Manners

Mailing Mama

YOU ARE JUST NOT GOING TO BELIEVE WHAT I AM ABOUT to tell you, so I'm just going to swear right now that I did not make up one word of this story, nor have I exaggerated a single detail. I saw it with my own two eyes, and I still can't believe it happened.

You might think nothing interesting has happened at the post office since Miss Eudora Welty wrote about it, but you'd be wrong. Just this week, I was standing in line at the post office, minding my own business, when I overheard the customer in front of me describe the contents of the package she was mailing.

"No, it isn't fragile or hazardous," she reassured the postmistress, who is required by law to ask those sorts of questions, you know.

Then she added, voluntarily, of her own free will, as if she wasn't the least little bit ashamed to say this in front of God and everyone in line at the post office: "It's the cremated remains of my mother."

As you can imagine, every single person in line sucked in one collective gasp of air and took two steps back from the window. It was as if we had all decided, as one body, to get as far away as possible from someone who might clearly be struck down by a vengeful bolt of lightning at any moment. If that woman had spontaneously combusted like someone right off the Discovery Channel, I would not have been any more surprised.

That's right. There's no need to reread that paragraph. You read it correctly. That woman was mailing her mother's ashes to her sister in a town an hour's drive away, and she didn't seem a bit squeamish about it. Carrying her dead mother's ashes into the post office like a mail order of pistachio nuts didn't strike this woman as unseemly, freakish, or horribly inappropriate at all. I was getting nauseous just standing behind her in line, but she seemed completely calm about the whole shebang.

Why, you may ask, since you were probably reared much more sensitively than this woman, was she mailing her mama's ashes to her sister who lived a mere hour's drive away?

Brazen heathen that she obviously was, she volunteered an answer to that unasked question, as well. She told the postmistress that it was "more convenient than having to drive them over there personally." Yes, ma'am, that's right. I'm telling you she said that out loud, in public, where we all could hear, without a whiff of embarrassment.

I had to step out of line and collect myself. I was completely, totally, utterly flummoxed. My imagination had shifted to warp speed, and I was imagining her sister walking out to the mailbox in a couple of days, sorting through the bills, sale circulars, and catalogs and stumbling on her mama's ashes. She says to herself, "Well, I guess my sister finally got her act together and mailed Mama's ashes to me so I can do something with them."

I can only assume that kind of behavior is acceptable in that family. Who knows? Maybe that mama knew her good-for-nothing, lazy, cold-fish daughters wouldn't be able to go to the trouble of planning a full-scale funeral, so she opted for cremation instead, hoping they could pull that off for her without too much fuss. Obviously, she failed to specify what she wanted done with her ashes.

Somehow, I doubt that a quick swing through the post-office doors on her way to eternity was what she had in mind.

I can tell you for sure that my mama would not take kindly to that sort of treatment. There would be one mad mama ghost dogging the footsteps of my sister and me until the end of our days, and we would deserve every scary minute of it.

"Happens all the time," the postmistress told me as I staggered back through the post-office doors, still a little dazed and wondering what this world is coming to. Although I am a bossy Southern woman who generally has an opinion about what should be done in any situation, I couldn't think of a thing to do for that mama except to say a prayer for her, which I did. While I was at it, I threw in a little prayer for the two daughters. I think they needed it.

Taking Turns With Strangers

I AM APPALLED TO REPORT THAT SEEMINGLY intelligent adults in our communities appear to have forgotten how to wait in line politely. I'm tempted to allow my daughter to record a public service announcement that we could play on the radio to teach people how to take turns nicely. Most of us learned how to take turns on the playground, waiting for our turn in the swings—something along those lines—but, apparently, some children never had to share, and it's causing problems for the rest of us now that they've grown up to be selfish, self-absorbed adults.

Some grown-ups seem to average about one nanosecond of patience. Their attention spans are about the length of a fast-food commercial. I'm not even going to address the martyred sighing, the relentless whining, or the rage that is an entirely inappropriate response to a short delay in restaurant seating or traffic merging that we all witness on a daily basis. You have to wonder: Did none of these people have brothers or sisters? Did they play team sports? Do they have any social skills whatsoever? It seems like some adults go through life as supersized two-year-olds, playing side by side but not exactly interacting with other adults.

Clearly, some adults need a time-out. Have you ever watched the adult version of a temper tantrum thrown by a grown-up who feels valet parking is taking a little too long?

I once saw an old man literally stamp his feet, throw his keys, and let fly with a stream of obscenities—all because the valet parking attendant couldn't get his car out for him fast enough. All I could think about was the fact that I'd just watched the man consume enough beef on a plate to clog his arteries for life, and his temper tantrum could only stress his heart even further. We'd never even met, and I wanted to slap his face. I figured if heart disease didn't end up killing him, a parking attendant just might. He certainly had it coming to him.

Grown-ups who routinely pay exorbitant fees for private trainers to personalize exercise routines for them crowd the valet stand like salmon trying to squeeze upstream in time to lay eggs before they die. As you might guess, I'm not a valet parking kind of person. I don't have the temperament for it. I didn't allow my children to throw temper tantrums. Watching an adult have a fit—without appropriate repercussions—is not something I care to do.

I've seen perfectly healthy adults who say they need king-sized beds and bathrooms the size of my first living room, the same adults who cry about the lack of space on aircraft seats, crowd others in front of them in line at the ice-cream stand with a total disregard for personal space. They act like they're lining up for their last meal on earth. When waiting in line for a vanilla cone, I should not have to suffer bodily injury from hefty handbags slung about in my vicinity. I should not have to dodge the sticky hands of children I did not give birth to, and there is only so much buffeting and jostling from men a hundred pounds heavier than I am that I can take before I start to take those shoves personally.

Next time you're waiting in line, I'd like you to take a deep breath. Look on it as an opportunity to meet and greet those around you, or, if that isn't appealing, go ahead and eavesdrop on your neighbors. You might hear something interesting. At the very least, it'll give you something to gossip about over dinner.

Borrowing Treasures

MOST SOUTHERN FAMILIES HAVE AT LEAST ONE treasured possession that is passed down through the generations and back and forth among dear friends. Sometimes, the family treasure really is a fine antique worth a bundle of bucks, but it could just as easily be something of great sentimental but little monetary value.

One of the great joys in a Southern woman's life is owning something worthy of borrowing, and there is no sweeter music to her ears than having one of her favorite pieces of silver, jewelry, or china referred to as a "must have" for an upcoming social event in her community.

In our heart of hearts, most of us Southern women are thrifty. Notice I didn't say cheap. Semantic distinctions are important. "Thrifty" is a virtue. "Cheap" is tacky, plain and simple. I think the thrifty trait is some sort of genetic mutation in survivors of the Civil War that allowed our ancestors to hang on to the family silver we're using today, as opposed to selling it to some carpetbagger, without starving to death in the process.

For example, it is true that most Southern women expect their children and grandchildren to be christened in yards and yards of exquisite linen or cotton and row after row of handmade lace—in gowns that are such hand-sewn works of art it won't matter how unattractive the infant is. However, most of those women see no reason in the world why they should have to pay for all that fine needlework when someone in the family already owns one of those gowns that has been passed down for generations. Family budgets these days don't usually cover christening-gown purchases that exceed monthly mortgage payments.

These women know it is wise to call the matriarch who has custody of the heirloom christening gown from the delivery room of the hospital to reserve that gown for a christening date six months down the road. When you get multiple generations of cousins sharing one christening gown, it's best to book the gown in advance or plan your pregnancy according to dress availability. After all, that baby will grow up and pierce her ear five times or her eyebrow twice or get a tattoo, but those christening photographs are going to be around forever.

I have a friend from Mobile, Alabama, who swears his family punch bowl has been to more wedding receptions than most Mobilians. I reminded him that it is an honor to have a punch bowl that Mobilians (a city chock-full of women who take their sterling silver seriously) want to borrow, and the fact that one might hear a cousin announce, "Catherine is engaged!" followed by, "Good! I'll bring the punch bowl!" from the matriarch is really confirmation that all is well in the world of Southern women.

It is just a shame and an unfortunate fact of life that in the twenty-first century we do not all have access to sterling-silver luxuries like punch bowls, but that does not mean we don't all *want* one. We've just learned to make do with really fine crystal.

I also reminded my friend that his family's punch bowl is sterling silver, weighs more than a river barge, and would require an armed guard in most countries in the world. Here in the South, of course, it's frequently loaded into the back of an old lady's car along with branches of freshly cut magnolia limbs, French wired ribbon, and pruning shears for a final touches trip to the reception site before a wedding.

Forget real estate, I advised my friend, ask for the punch bowl for your inheritance. I believe he could make a nice living just renting that dinosaur out.

In case you're wondering, I'm just kidding about renting out the punch bowl to strangers. I would never, ever do that, of course. Half the fun of owning a family heirloom is getting to decide who may or may not borrow it. And they say vengeance only belongs to the Lord. Remember that when you pick on your fat cousin. Odds are she may one day control the calendar for the family punch bowl, lace tablecloth, christening font, beach cottage, or diamond brooch. You know how sweet revenge can be. If you don't mind your manners at an early age, your future children may find themselves eating off silver plate and being baptized in cheap lace—all because you called your cousin Fat Frances in fifth grade. As far as I know, there is no statute of limitations on fat jokes among Southern women.

You really know you've *arrived* as a friend when family treasures are offered to you, a non-family member, for important occasions in your own life. There is just no nicer token of friendship than, "Of course, you must borrow mother's pearls for the wedding." Now, if you have one lick of sense, you know to immediately decline gracefully and gratefully. No way do you want to be remembered forever in that family as the idiot who lost, broke, stole, dropped, sat on, or threw up on the family heirloom.

Sure, in general, friendship is more important than any material possession, and that philosophy works fine with silver plate, but with sterling, it's an entirely different ball game.

Overheard in a Crowd

BECAUSE GOD HAS A SENSE OF HUMOR AND AMUSED himself in the 1990s by sending children who love sports to grow to adulthood in my house, I have spent a depressing number of hours trapped in boring, hot, cramped, unforgiving concrete and metal ballpark bleachers and stadium seats. In my martyred seating, I have been regularly shocked by the indiscrete, loud, obviously private and personal conversations swirling around my ears involving complete strangers. These individuals engage in colorful dialogue I cannot possibly avoid overhearing, even if I stick my fingers in my ears, hum loudly to myself, and rattle my program like I'm swatting house flies. In self-defense, I have learned that nothing clears out some bench space on a bleacher faster than loud speculation along the lines of, "I hope I'm not still contagious."

This kind of embarrassing talk has led me to believe that those of us interested in maintaining minimum standards of social constraints and some semblance of civility in our interactions with strangers in public places need to be more explicit about what are acceptable conversation topics for all those loudmouth discussions that can be—and will be—overheard, puzzled over, and recounted gleefully at dinner parties for the next ten years by all those within a stone's throw distance. (Don't think I'm ruling out that old-testament stoning punishment as a fitting end for some of the filthy mouths I've been forced to listen to because I am certainly *not*. When did a trashy mouth become socially acceptable?)

I've overheard profanity from the mouths of adults seated near us in restaurants that was so blue I had to lean over and ask my husband for definitions and explanations. I've watched movies where teenagers refer to body parts I don't think appear in the big book of *Gray's Anatomy*. I have found myself casting filthy looks at perfect strangers standing near me in line to encourage them to edit their language so my children won't be subjected to a complete pornographic education before they reach puberty.

Personally, I have always considered profanity a sign of laziness. I routinely tell my children that profanity is a sign of stupidity. Only those with tiny brains and limited vocabularies have to resort to vulgarities, I argue. Wouldn't it be sad if you were that stupid? I'm thinking of packing a few paperback thesauruses in my big purse. As a public service, I could pass them out to those in dire need of a little Scrabble help. In one single act of philanthropy, I could improve the vocabulary of average Americans and encourage family friendly social interaction. It just doesn't get any better than that.

If your mother was too busy washing dishes, folding laundry, and keeping up with your exhausting adolescent self to explain such conversational pitfalls to you early on, let me connect the dots for you as an adult: some topics are best addressed in the privacy of your own home. In all honesty, some topics are best left entirely alone. Who needs extra trouble? If you are the mistaken recipient of a mail-order catalog for sex toys, there is just no reason in the world for you to bring that to the ballpark for a detailed examination in between innings. Remember what happened to that curious cat. Legally speaking, that kind of reading material is just an attractive nuisance. Somebody in the stands is just bound to be too busy reading over your shoulder to avoid getting smacked in the kisser by a fly ball.

If you are seated in close proximity to others in a movie theater, on a stadium bleacher, or in the cheap seats of a live play, the rest of us do not need to hear about your personal problems. Your minute-by-minute recitation of your menopause symptoms, while obviously enthralling to you, does nothing for the rest of us. Ditto any discussion of your prostate difficulties. Ugh. The painful details of your recent foray into bikini waxing are mental images we could all live without. If you persist in publicly discussing such intimate details, you can expect a traffic jam at the end of your row of seats as eavesdroppers crane their necks trying to get a glimpse of your indiscrete face when the lights come on and they file past for intermission.

You should know that many of us have come out into a public setting to escape such unpleasant intimate discussions in our own homes. We have no interest in hearing about your cheating spouses, gastrointestinal peculiarities, or your are-they-real-or-fake body-part debates. We've heard it all before. We have friends and families, too, you know. We all need a break from our more-interesting-than-soap-opera lives.

We would actually prefer not to be subjected to the same base discussions from your point of view. In the first place, we don't care what you think. About anything. In the second place, we will undoubtedly become fascinated by your tales of daytime-talk-show shenanigans, and we will be distracted from whatever it is that is going on in our own lives that must, obviously, be more lofty and important. We will become intensely frustrated when our good manners prevent us from swiveling around in our seats to stare at you to see if you can possibly be as ignorant, uneducated, stupid, poorly read, and irritatingly uninformed as you sound.

Most frustrating of all is the fact that we will not be able to offer you our own inspired solutions to your problems because we don't know you. These solutions will, no doubt, be patently obvious to us since they are your problems and not our own much more complex, multi-layered, unique, and special-circumstances kind of problems. We fear that you may be mentally unstable or a gun-packing kind of gal with an inclination to shoot first and ask questions later, so we will be forced to fume silently with the occasional eye roll or hissed breath as our only reaction to whatever foolish nonsense you are pouring out of your mouth into the universe.

As everyone knows, there is nothing in the world more difficult for a Southern woman to do than to keep her mouth shut—even in potentially life-threatening situations. It would not surprise me a bit to find a Southern woman in an emergency room who is willing to admit, even after being shot, "Yeah, it hurt, but it was worth it. I've been dying to say that for years." Teddy Roosevelt said, "I was always willing to pay the piper when I have had a good dance." We believe that, too, Teddy.

You know why this sort of bawdy rhetoric has become such a problem? Lack of self-restraint. Think about it. We have become a culture that does anything and says anything without a single thought about the consequences, large or small. I find this rise in the socially acceptable obscenity level amazing in light of the current trend of politically correct speech. I'm offended all the time; don't I count? I guess the PC police aren't too worried about my Southern-woman demographic sensibilities. Why doesn't that surprise me?

What we need is a little more filtering. We should all think like State Department diplomats addressing the two-China semantic distinction between the People's Republic of China and Taiwan. Rogue province or sovereign nation? Depends on where you live. *Words matter.*

I'm as guilty as the next person. I loved watching *Sex and the City*, even though I had to sit with my head right next to the television to hear it. I couldn't turn the volume up with children in the house because every third word was an obscenity. We've become a culture that adds profanity to our sentences as space fillers (along with the ever-popular, maddening, "like" and "anyway," a new millennium version of "um").

I'm horrified. We've got to do better. Otherwise, we're going to have ten-month-old babies babbling, "Mama, I want my —— pacifier!" While I might actually enjoy saying, "Move your fat fanny over. You are taking up my stadium seat as well as your own," I won't. That's the beauty of having nice manners. I try to be considerate of other people even when I don't really mean it. We should all fake it more often. There's a lot to be said for that.

Ten Things I am Never Going to Do Before I Die

It seems that not a week goes by that I don't hear people going on and on about the list of things they want to do before they die. First of all, I can't help but wonder why those people are thinking such morbid thoughts in the first place. Surely, all those people aren't knocking on death's door. Next, I wonder how they have time in the middle of the day to ponder about such things. I barely have time to make a grocery list—much less a thoughtful, soul-searching, poignant wish list to map out the rest of my days. Mercy!

Instead, I find myself mentally adding entries to an ongoing list of things I am *never* going to do. This list doesn't require one bit of deep thinking. Try it yourself. If you're like me, you can fire off a top-ten list on this subject while you're waiting for a traffic light to turn green. My list of things I am never going to do before I die, thus far, is:

1) Travel to countries without public restrooms. I'm so over that.

2) Get a tattoo. I just don't get it. One person's tattoo is another person's birthmark. I ask you: How many attractive tattoos have you seen on old people? None, I'm willing to bet.

3) Give up chocolate. All things are possible in moderation, you know.

4) Sunbathe. It's just not worth the price anymore.

5) Pierce anything else. One hole in each ear is enough for me.

6) Adopt any more animals. I MEAN it this time.

7) Ride in the backseat of a car if it is not a life-threatening emergency. I get carsick. Somebody else will have to climb over.

8) Bring home any more babies to live at our house—no matter how much I am tempted. The inn is full. I'm not sure I can afford to educate the children I have.

9) Sit behind someone in a movie theater who talks throughout the movie. I'll just move. Video rentals have spoiled me. Occasionally, I like to see an epic production on the big screen. Unfortunately, I have to view it with the masses.

10) Drive across town to save a dollar on laundry detergent. My time is worth at least a dollar.

Southern Mamas and Sports

Southern Mamas and Sports

WHY DID GOD SEND ME THREE CHILDREN WHO love sports? What was he thinking? I don't think I'm a very athletically inclined person, but I don't really know. I'll never know because when I was growing up in south Alabama, there weren't many opportunities for girls to play sports. I'm glad that's not true anymore. The opportunities that were available were often second rate. There was an accepted mentality that said, "Sure, girls can have a team. They can use the gym when the boys are finished." The most competitive girls' team in my high school played basketball. They were named the Dolls. That just about sums it up, doesn't it?

In fact, if I remember correctly, grownup women were only allowed to play golf on the local course on one day of the week. Can you imagine enforcing that rule today? It reminds me of photographs depicting two water fountains in the South—one for African Americans and one for whites. I'm relieved to say I'm too young to remember that reality, but to this day, I'm just amazed that everyone didn't jump up and say, "What in the world? Have you lost your minds?" History shows us it's scary what people can get used to and accept as normal.

My daughter has a strong sense of social justice, too. Her class is made up of an ethnically diverse group of children. Their class picture looks like an ad campaign extolling the virtues of diversity. When a girl of Chinese ancestry in my daughter's class explained the traditional worth of girl babies verses boy babies in China to my child, my daughter came home so indignant and outraged I thought we were going to have to write a formal letter of diplomatic protest to shut her up. She caught on pretty fast that in some countries in the world, her brothers would be considered more desirable in a family. I'm here to tell you that piece of information was hard for her to swallow.

Suffice it to say that Title Nine wasn't even an academic discussion when I was in school. It is, therefore, *possible* that I had great athletic talent that was just wasted because I was born with two *X* chromosomes. However, I'll be the first to admit it is merely a theoretical possibility for a hypothetical discussion. Even if I had been born with great athletic talent that was subsequently squandered by Southern society in general, I have to admit it wouldn't have made a bit of difference. It wouldn't have mattered if I'd been offered a spot on a United States Olympic team. The truth is that I don't like to get hot and sweaty, and most sports I've seen just thrive on having participants get hot and sweaty—a real deal killer for me. Bottom line: we'll never know what I might have accomplished, if anything, on the athletic field, but my children seem to be making up for all the sports I didn't try. They're into them *all*.

For the first few years when my children played sports, I kept waiting to get back to my life. I was always just trying to keep everything together in the rest of our lives to limp to the end of the season. One day when I was sitting in the stands, I had a sports epiphany. Of course, I stood up to shout my epiphany to the world (all the parents seated near me, anyway). *"HEY!* It is *always* going to be some season or another! This isn't going to end for years and years! This could go on through college!" I then collapsed in my stadium seat, appalled at my newly discovered reality and exhausted by the weight of it.

"Yes, of course," my more experienced friends responded, "we thought you knew."

My three children love to play and watch a variety of sports. They think that's fun. Since they make good grades in school, and sports keep them exercising their bodies rather than stagnating in front of the television, video games, or a computer screen, I can't really think of a reasonable parental objection to their participation. What I didn't expect is how much participating *I* would have to do.

As a result, I find myself sitting for hours and hours in hot, sweaty ballparks or freezing my behind in stadiums all over the state. I spend more money on questionable food products at concession stands than I do at fine restaurants. Last year, my husband and I went wild and split an order of chicken fingers in the bottom of the ninth inning to celebrate our anniversary.

With three children playing sports all year, there is not one single day of the week when no one has a practice or a game. Every day, it is a challenge to get homework done, uniforms clean, equipment ready, and still maintain some semblance of family life. When one team makes it to the play-offs, sport seasons overlap, and no one is happy. Coaches often behave as if their baby football, baseball, or basketball players are professionals with nothing else to do but focus on the team. As parents, we try to keep our children balanced. Sure, I've dressed a kid in his baseball uniform to play in his piano recital. Hasn't everyone? We try to make it all work. Sometimes it's hard. Thanks to overzealous adults, often it is needlessly complicated.

Usually, men run the sports leagues. That means they often schedule games to begin at night when responsible parents usually tuck their children in bed. I've learned not to let coaches run my life or the lives of my children, but they try, oh, yes, they try. Sometimes I think coaches are reliving their own frustrated childhoods. Moms like me have to watch out for that kind of silly thinking. Usually, for example, coaches play to win. Children, on the other hand, play for fun. They rarely remember the score.

What I did not expect when my children began playing sports were the jobs that I would be assigned. It's not enough to write a check for each child that is more money than I spend entertaining myself in an entire year. I can safely assume that I'll be assigned snack duty, concession work, ticket sales, tournament preparation, fund-raising, and any other grunt work for which I am clearly over-educated and under-enthused to perform.

If I paid dues to a trucker's union, I wouldn't be allowed to drive this many hours, schlepping kids back and forth to practices and games. If you haven't parented a couple of athletic boys and girls with overlapping schedules, you cannot comprehend the logistics involved. If I worked as my kids' nanny, I'd be richer than Midas. We couldn't afford to pay me by the hour.

Children's sports activities give you a whole new perspective on the professional teams you love to watch. For example, when I watch a team of baseball players take the field, all I see is laundry. I may never as long as I live get over the pressure of constantly trying to wash red mud out of white baseball pants. Lady Macbeth's hand-wringing fantasy blood was nothing compared to Alabama red clay. During all-star seasons, my kids frequently wear identical jerseys. Only the numbers are different. You better believe I've put the wrong jersey on a kid and screwed up some lineups. In my opinion, that is a perfectly understandable mistake.

My kids eagerly anticipate the name of their basketball, baseball, football, and soccer teams every year. Usually kids' park-league teams mirror professional teams, so you could have a five-year-old Laker or a ten-year-old Yankee living in your home, for example. I'm always anxious to know what color the jerseys will be. That color determines what kind of bleach or bleach alternative I'll need to stock in my stain-removing arsenal to face the current season's Gatorade drooling emergencies.

When my kids first see the team roster at the beginning of the season, they scan the list quickly for the names of their friends, ringers, and automatic outs. I look to see whose parents I'll be sharing the bleachers with for three or four months. I don't care whether the team has a winning or losing season. I want to know if any of my friends are going to be sharing my joys and sorrows from the sidelines. Plus, I need to see if there is another mother or father on the team who I can trust to use seatbelts to transport my child on the inevitable three-children-playing-at-the-same-time evenings.

On the upside, I've now learned a thing or two about sports. The first thing I learned is not to bring a book to read. Apparently, that is very offensive. Without even realizing it, I've picked up strange little tidbits of information, and they come out at odd times. I once walked through a hotel lobby, dressed in evening attire and waiting on my husband to join me. Two men were watching a baseball game and puzzling over a strange call.

"Balk," I said, as I passed them.

"Excuse me," said one, "Did you just say 'squawk' to me?"

"No," I replied, "I said 'balked.' The pitcher balked. He should have just gone ahead and thrown it."

"Dang. I think she's right," the other guy said, obviously surprised. A little sports trivia can be helpful in certain social situations in the South. I admit it.

One great thing about having athletic children and knowing nothing about the sports they're involved in is that I don't bring any personal prejudices, bad experiences, or know-it-all parent mentality to my kids' games. All of the prejudices I now have I learned through personal observation.

I've figured out that coaches come in three types: those who know a lot about the sport, those who work well with kids, and those who have adult people skills. The very best coaches, of course, combine all three characteristics, but they are very, very rare. Everyone knows that a great coach can change the course of a kid's life. The worst coaches can hurt their feelings so much they never forget the experience. I've seen them all.

My kids have been lucky. Their team experiences have been mostly positive. I've watched them take note of every word those coaches say, and I've seen them take the measure of the men coaching them. Like all of us, adults sometimes disappoint them. We've had some late night conversations about that.

My kids have learned major life lessons by playing sports. They know: how to win and lose gracefully; how to choose between personal glory and team glory; how to make the worst kid on their team look good in at least one game; how to handle hot-tempered adults and children; how to be a good sport; how to never give up; how to reach down and dig deeper when they're hurt, tired, or feeling unwell; how to handle pressure; how to tag their friends out at home base and then help them up to their feet and pat them on the back; how to use their time wisely (because they know they're not going to play unless their school work is completed first); how to spread credit around to the whole team; how to encourage others—no matter how long the odds are; how to sacrifice for friends; how to be a kind person and a tough competitor at the same time; how to handle jealousy; how to ignore sideline taunts; and how to react to adults who behave badly. In short, team sports have taught my children how to handle life.

I guess that makes it all worth it. I still envy people who are going out to dinner and a movie this weekend. So far, we have four games scheduled. For me, the jury is still out on this one. I'll let you know.

Overheard in the Stands

I can't get over what people say in public places. It's shocking. I have overheard comments from the mouths of strangers that *should* have embarrassed them half to death but, apparently, did not. Well, I am embarrassed *for* them. Somebody should be. Here's a sampling of the choice tidbits I have heard strangers share with the world at large:

"I can tell they're fake from all the way over here."

"If he thinks I'm sleeping with him after that, he better think again!"

"It's not really stealing. Everybody does it."

"Do you think that crab dip was bad? I spent the whole night in the bathroom!"

"I don't know what you're making such a fuss about. I put it back in the safe. I was just looking at it."

"She has the worst bad breath in the world."

"I don't think the police ever found out about it, or he wouldn't be allowed to coach."

"I don't know what you're so upset about. It's not loaded."

"Did I tell you about my last surgery? They gutted me like a fish."

"I don't know whose car I backed into. I didn't hang around to find out."

"I don't think we should see each other any more after this."

"Glad to see you! We're all sick as dogs at our house. I shouldn't even be here."

"Just put a Band-Aid over it. No one will notice."

"How is that any of your business?"

"If we sneak out now, no one will even know."

Bite Your Tongue

WHENEVER I CAN, I LIKE TO SAVE MY READERS FROM suffering through any incidents of public humiliation I have personally endured myself. I consider this one of my personal responsibilities and a matter of good citizenship. Over the years, I am sad to report that I have, indeed, made a number of statements about sports that did not go down very well with sports-savvy audiences. I'd hate to see you repeat my mistakes.

However, if you are one of those women who knows all the rules in football, basketball, baseball, hockey, tennis, golf, and all the rest, and you can translate what the referee is saying, well, then, I say more power to you. I'm a little bit jealous. Also, I would really appreciate it if you could sit by me at the next game because I spend a lot of time saying things like: "What was that? What did he do? What does that mean? Is that a big deal? Is he in trouble? Why is that other player mad? Can the coach DO that? Did she do that on purpose? Is he going to the locker room or jail?" Honestly, I could use the help.

I've always secretly wished that professional players had microphones attached to their jerseys like those preachers you see on Sunday morning television. I'd love to hear what they're saying to each other on the field. That would really spice up the boring parts for me. I bet there's some juicy conversation in the huddle. Of course, we'd need one of those censor buttons to listen to the live feed because I bet the language used out there would be right at home in an episode of *The Sopranos*.

If you're like me, you're not well informed about sports in general, but your lifestyle, and the husband and children who live with you, require at least token participation and appreciation of every sports season, regardless of your individual preferences. Think of it like the Olympics. Sometimes, you can get interested in watching a sport you didn't even know existed until they show it on television. Had you ever heard of curling before the Olympics? I tell you it was new to me.

Also, just so you know, it is always some sports season or other, and the seasons invariably overlap because of tournaments and bowl games and poor planning, apparently, by the men who run such things. The dueling sports weeks often cause great consternation in our family. This is information you won't get from your kid's coach, so I'm giving you fair warning right now. The fact that your son or daughter will have basketball games and baseball practice in the same week is just one of the many things you're supposed to *just know*. In addition, there will be more games and practices in reality than are actually printed on the photocopied handout you get from the coach at the parent meeting on the first day. Don't go entering those dates in pen on your calendar, and don't shell out any non-refundable vacation rental deposits. Your weekend can go from big-city fine dining and drinks with adult friends to hot dogs with snotty-nosed kids in a ballpark in the middle of nowhere in a New York minute. You need to prepare yourself now. It will save you from so many crushed dreams later.

There are other things nobody tells you about. For example, you can count on adding at least a week of practice before the "official" beginning of the season and at least a week or so after. Don't be silly enough to plan any family vacations during school holidays either. Heck, you'll be lucky if you see a movie on the big screen again. And if you have more than one child playing at the same time, you can forget sitting down as a family to eat dinner in the foreseeable future. Your toddler could starve to death waiting on a big brother to get home from football practice.

Another little quirk in the sporting world is that, frequently, you'll only be told when practice is scheduled to *begin.* You won't know when it will end; the coach will only say they are going to practice "an hour or two," so if you have multiple kids, work, a life that you're trying to schedule, you'll never be able to plan when to arrive so your kid isn't left waiting alone on a field for you to pick him or her up before a pedophile comes by or lightning strikes. You often get to wait on one of your children while standing in the corner of the gym calling out spelling words to one of your other kids. If it's a particularly difficult week, and you left one child at home throwing up so you could pick up the sibling, "an hour or two" really doesn't pin things down quite enough to be helpful. Big sigh.

It's hard to be the mama of athletes.

Don't be surprised if your middle-school-aged kid's baseball coach thinks that a thirteen-year-old baseball game is more important than your sister's wedding. When the football coach schedules spring training to conflict with baseball practice—and he will—don't expect the two adult coaches to work that out among themselves. Oh, no. It will be up to your kid to "decide what is most important to him." Stunning, but true.

Another thing you can count on: the math teacher is going to schedule every major test the day after an away ball game. There are a lot of petty power struggles that go on between teachers and coaches. Guess who gets caught in the middle? That's right. Your kid.

If you are a sports-challenged parent like me, I'm trying to save you a little grief today. I suggest you review the following list to see if it might help you avoid making any embarrassing sports statements of your own. You know how much we embarrass our teenagers by continuing to live and breathe. I'd hate for you to stick your cleat in your mouth as I have done many, many times. A few minutes of reading now could save you from public ridicule later. Trust me.

My all-time most embarrassing sports remarks, so far:

In the middle of the Super Bowl: "Do you think the players have to wash their own uniforms?"

On the same obsessive laundry subject, my contribution to a heated debate between two of my friends over the advantages of natural verses artificial turf: "I don't care if there are fewer injuries on natural grass. Do you have any *idea* how hard grass stains are to remove?"

Watching a college football game: "I can guarantee you that if someone wanted a small leather ball from me bad enough to knock me down for it, I'd just give it to him. It's the same premise as giving up your purse without a fight to a mugger."

On the stealing that goes on in basketball: "I really think they should let him finish his turn before they snatch the ball away like that. It's rude."

Watching college coaches yell at their players on the sidelines: "If I'd yelled at a college student in one of my English classes for not turning in an essay the way that coach is yelling at that boy for missing a tackle, I'd have been fired—maybe arrested!"

Watching my first children's soccer match: "I think this game should be called 'running up and down the field with your friends.'"

Watching my first state-final wrestling match: "Is this sport legal? I think this may be assault and battery!"

Watching a basketball coach allow his starting lineup to run up the score on a team with no talent: "This is just terribly bad manners."

After watching the inevitable collision when a third-base runner tries to steal home in baseball: "Don't they have to take turns? We're just asking for a trip to the emergency room here!"

Watching a championship basketball game: "What do you mean there can be more than one overtime? This game is over! I know; I sat through the whole darn thing!"

Watching the final two holes in a golf tournament: "Finally! A sport I can appreciate. You go for a long walk, finish with drinks in the club house, and hand out cash prizes."

Playing with the Big Boys

ONCE YOUR CHILDREN REACH A CERTAIN AGE, ABOUT the time they can look you in the eye, a startling thing happens. It's perfectly natural. It's entirely predictable. Like many perfectly natural and entirely predictable happenings, it seems unbelievable when it happens in your own life. My sweet baby boys are growing up. They're my size now, and they're not even in high school yet. As you might imagine, they are already more skilled than I am in every athletic endeavor.

They're younger, stronger, faster, and better trained. They're not carrying around an extra ten pounds at the waistline, and they aren't the least bit worried about brittle bones. They still believe they are immortal, and they don't have an adult's fear of pain because their life experiences have been remarkably healthy, smooth sailing, thus far. These are boys who can eat a bag of Oreos, wash it down with half a gallon of milk, and follow that with four slices of pizza without a pang of guilt. Of course, when I was their age, I could do that, too, and I'm sad to report that I didn't appreciate it any more than they do. These days, what I would like to do to a big bag of Doritos would make a hungry dog blush.

It amazes me that the little darlings I first rolled and then threw balls to—gently, underhanded—are now too dangerous to play catch with unless I have on protective gear like police officers would don to wade into a riot. There was a time when my kids loved to throw the baseball with me. I'd mix up pop flies, grounders, and line drives, and I'd embroider our play with colorful play-by-play commentary that set them up for one game-winning catch after another. Every kid in the world loves to imagine him or herself as the hero. It is only a few years later—although it seems like about ten minutes—but now I agree to throw with them only if they promise not to throw too hard. "Anything coming at me at the speed of a game pitch, and I'm out of here, and you can kiss dessert goodbye tonight," I warn them.

One of my proudest parenting moments occurred when one of my children's friends asked my son, a trifle askance, "You're going to warm up with your *mother*?" Thankfully, my child didn't look a bit embarrassed, "Oh, yeah. You should see her. She's old, but she doesn't throw like a girl. My mom has an *arm*." Yes, I do believe that is the highest athletic praise I have ever received. I enjoy that moment again every time I think about it.

Recently, I was asked to play a game of one-on-one basketball with my oldest son. I agreed cautiously, and only after some tournament rule negotiating in my favor.

"First, you have to spot me fifteen points, or I'm not playing," I demanded, matter-of-factly.

My son looked appalled at my not-playing-unless-things-go-my-way sportsmanship, an attitude he knew to be strictly forbidden in our backyard. *"Fifteen?* Don't you think that's a little greedy, Mom?"

"No, I don't," I responded, not feeling guilty at all. "Also, I get to travel all over the place, and whenever my shots go in, they're all three-pointers," I added, with a final stroke of sneaky brilliance.

You guessed it. I was trying to even out the match a little. In other words, my game plan involved flagrant cheating. It was my only chance.

I played to win. I charged right through the boy I gave birth to. I reached in and slapped his hands to knock the ball out. When he was going in for an easy lay-up, I stuck my foot out and tripped him.

"FOUL! FOUL! That was clearly a *FOUL! MOM*, you can't *DO* THAT!" my son screamed, incensed at the home cooking going on in our game.

"Sure I can!" I screamed back. "You want some of this?" I asked, making my lay-up and scoring my only basket of the day.

He let me have it then. He showed no mercy. I was shellacked, and I had it coming. Obviously, the taunting was one step too far in my strategy. My little psych-him-out mind game didn't work. Apparently, he'd heard about that one before.

Eventually, I had to feign injury. I hit the patio, going for an Oscar performance, clutching my ankle. "Son, I'm hurt."

He approached cautiously, sensing a trap. "You're not even bleeding. Get up and finish the game."

Craftily (I thought), I shot the ball over his shoulder when he bent down to check on my ankle.

Flashing that smile that I have loved since the day he was born, my son said, "You are the biggest cheater I ever saw, Mom."

"I prefer to think of myself as a creative strategist," I answered.

My son snorted.

Whoever thought it could be so much fun to lose?

You Shouldn't Be a Little-League Umpire If . . .

You give the players more free advice than the coaches do.

No one would guess you ever played baseball yourself.

You have a hard time throwing the ball hard enough to
get it back to the pitcher.

You love baseball but dislike small children.

You have ever been forced to attend anger-management classes.

You sweat so much in navy blue that you drip on the catcher.

You are so overweight you cast a looming
shadow over the batter's box.

You have the social skills of a baboon and the backside
to express yourself equally colorfully.

You are so thin-skinned that being called "bubble butt" from the sidelines results in a spectator being ejected from the ballpark.

You forget that a tie goes to the runner at home plate or,
in a 10-0 stomping, to the underdog.

You think your official baseball badge makes you
smarter than everybody else.

You are such a delicate, hothouse orchid you can't
ever admit to being wrong.

You forget that good kids sometimes have crummy parents.

You love the rules of baseball more than the
kids on both sides of the play.

You spend more time admiring the badge on your blue
shirt than you do watching the game.

The Old Woman Who Lived in the Shoe

Busy Days

HAVE YOU EVER HAD ONE OF THOSE DAYS WHEN YOU have so many things to do you can't decide what to do first, so you go off half-cocked in a thousand different directions, and, consequently, you never actually finish anything?

When I have one of those weeks that starts when I wake up at 3 AM on Monday morning to jot down another item on my to-do list so I won't forget it when I wake up, I know I'm working on brain overload.

Apparently, there is only so much available space inside my head. There is limited capacity seating, and storage availability is based on a first-come-first-served basis.

The first thing to go is my ability to prioritize. Thanks to the births of three children in five years, triage parenting is usually an area in which I excel. On one busy day, however, I'm ashamed to confess that I actually forced one of my children to finish copying his spelling words before I agreed to bandage his bleeding scraped knees. It made more sense time-wise than having him stop writing just for a little Band-Aid when I knew perfectly well it would take him forever to settle back into his homework again. I'm afraid my compassion is limited when we're under a homework deadline.

I always keep several lists going on the refrigerator so I can maintain a façade of togetherness as I trot well-worn weekly paths to the grocery store, ballpark, school, and church, but the façade has all the depth of a movie studio back-lot building and can't stand up to the first puff of wind from the big bad wolf.

One memorable day, for example, I took a hasty predawn shower, threw on some makeup and clothes, and the overall effect was normal, *unless* you noticed that for some inexplicable reason, I had only shaved one leg. Odd. Slightly disturbing. I have no idea why I did that.

In the middle of another busy day, I searched frantically for a child's birthday present I had purchased earlier and stockpiled in the gift closet in anticipation of a busy week. Yes, I put it up so I would know right where to find it when I needed it. Naturally, when I looked for it, I couldn't remember where I had stashed it. When I finally unearthed the small band of pirates and their ship, I found, in addition, a second set of pirates and ship, docked side by side on the same shelf. In other words, I bought the same present *twice*. I have no memory of doing that. Scary, isn't it?

I am a well-educated, reasonably intelligent person with a driver's license and primary care-taking responsibilities for three children, one cat, and ten fish, but I don't honestly know if it's safe to leave a self-sufficient houseplant in my care on a long-term basis.

The other day seemed doomed by a long list of distractions. It began innocently enough when I wiped off the kitchen counter after my kids ate their way through breakfast like African termites. There were toast crumbs trailing underneath their barstools like Hansel was marking his way home to Germany through an Alabama suburb. I was talking on the phone, organizing a school field trip (because, by definition, I am female and, therefore, required to multitask at all times), and, at the same time, I was sweeping up the crumbs, which brought me face-to-face with the dirtiest kitchen baseboards I've ever seen. I swear I think I saw some Kudzu branching up from the tracked-in soil on my hardwood floor.

Of course, those baseboards were nothing short of a cleaning emergency, so I got out the dust rags and hit the floor. When I got to the corner by the back door, I noticed the pitiful, half-dead flat of impatiens I bought two weeks ago, which were hanging on to life by a petal, and I decided to take five minutes to plant them in a big clay pot by my daughter's playhouse outside. That way she could water her very own flowers. Charming, I thought. Plus, they would add a much-needed spot of color to the backyard. Sadly, I remembered, we never got around to painting her playhouse in the wild, colorful, just-for-fun way we'd planned.

When I hung my gardening gloves up next to the shelf of old paint cans in the back shed, I couldn't help but notice all the leftover paint samples (*like a sign*) from my last foray into paint-chip-selection world. I was already dirty, so I figured it couldn't take me more than an hour to slap a coat of paint on the playhouse. I couldn't find a paintbrush, but I did find an old sponge and some rags that would do in a pinch to paint a house where squirrels, birds, and earthworms are invited in for tea parties.

Two hours later, I had to abandon the backyard to pick up my children from school, help them begin homework, cook supper, and drive to the ballpark, all with globs of brightly colored paint in my hair and on my hands and arms because we were out of paint remover—unless, of course, I'd put the paint remover up somewhere, and I'd forgotten where, an entirely possible event.

When I had to stop, there was one coat of paint on the playhouse. A few scraggly flowers were in pots. Half the kitchen baseboards were clean. There was congealed cereal left in the breakfast bowls in the sink. Not one job was finished properly. I was hot, tired, frustrated, and cranky.

It seems like my brain can only hold so much information, and when it gets full, it begins to overflow in all directions like an old lady's birdbath, with no discrimination or selectivity. Honestly, I'm afraid I'm going to wake up one busy morning and discover I've forgotten how to read because my brain suddenly realized it needed to free up some space and decided my whole phonics universe was just taking up way too much room.

Busy days make me feel like I'm running around like a chicken with its head cut off. I'm expending energy in all directions, but nothing is focused or directed. I'm working hard but not smart, as all the magazines warn us about. In other words, I am so busy doing *everything* that I accomplish *nothing*. (By the way, I looked up that chicken-with-its-head-cut-off simile, and I advise you not to do that unless you want a quick conversion to vegetarianism. I thought it conveyed a perfect mental image of what I'm going through, but I had no idea it was based on real life observation. I know the chicken that is shrink-wrapped at the Piggly Wiggly didn't commit suicide, but I need a little distance between me and the rest of the food chain. I'm never going to use that expression again. You shouldn't either. Trust me on this.)

I know what I need to do on those busy days. I need to slow down, think, prioritize, and maybe have a glass of wine. The important things will get done. They always do. The people who love me won't check the status of my kitchen baseboard filth, and if they do, well, I don't have time for them anyway.

I Quit

Most of the time, I like being a stay-at-home mom, and I feel lucky to be financially able to swing it. I think my children are better people because of it. Over the years, I've had lots of women say to me, "That just wasn't for me." "Me either," I always respond. I didn't do it for me. It didn't do my career one bit of good. I did it because I was able to do it, I'm good at it, and I believe it's good for my kids. Like any job, I agree that it's not for everyone. It's harder than any other job I have ever had. Also, like any other job I've ever worked, there are days when it just plain stinks. Stay-at-home moms like me get very little respect and no tangible rewards for the work we do. Some days are harder than others because parenting has lots of peaks and valleys. The following is a true story about one of my days in the valley.

I WANT TO QUIT MY JOB. RIGHT NOW. THIS VERY second. I don't want to work for these freakish people anymore. I used to enjoy my job, but I'm over it. In the words of a country song, you can "take this job and shove it. I aint working here no more." If you improve the grammar in those two sentences, they express my sentiments exactly. This is America. Nobody can *make* me work this job, right? I know I read that somewhere. This is a capitalist society. The problem is I can't find anyone to turn my huffy, whiny resignation letter in to.

Stay-at-home mothers like me need a union. I want to be first in line to talk to my union representative. Today. I'm ready to strike. I want reasonable hours, a paycheck, health insurance, a retirement account, disability . . . something that proves empirically that the society we live in values the work we do.

I want some respect. I don't want middle-school coaches to tell me to form a single-file line to pick up football equipment. I don't even play football. I do not want to be shushed by elementary-school teachers young enough to be my daughter while they explain to me for the third time in three years how the Popsicle behavior chart is going to work. I'm not worried about my children misbehaving in school. They know full well that if they get in trouble at school, they're going to be in twice as much trouble at home, and, besides, my children are more afraid of me than God Almighty. I'm not running a democracy around here. I run my household more along the lines of a benign dictatorship. I motivate the old-fashioned way—with fear, guilt, and love.

I believe that rearing kind, responsible, tax-paying citizens in my own little family is good for society as a whole. Hopefully, my children will grow up to be good employees and employers. They'll be tax-paying citizens who take care of their own families, show up for jury duty, and demonstrate a well-developed sense of responsibility for those less fortunate than themselves. That's the goal, and, so far, despite all that television, movies, and more permissive friends' parents can do to sabotage me, my kids are turning out to be nice people.

In case you haven't heard, I'm here to tell you that child-rearing is a JOB, and, right now, I'm fed up with it. If parenting is a series of peaks and valleys, I've fallen so far in a crevice that I can no longer see the surface of the earth. I'm dangling in the dark, holding on to the edge with my fingertips, and I could fall into oblivion at any minute. I've lost my perspective. I've lost confidence in the fact that what I am doing makes a difference. All I've got left is a smarty-pants sense of humor.

Right now I want to quit and do something else. Anything else. I'll work the cash register at a convenience store. I like ICEEs. I'll chop up vegetables for the primate house at the zoo. (Look it up. Primates eat an enormous quantity of vegetables every single day. It's a real job.) I'll work in a parking deck. I've always thought that would be a fabulous job. I'd read books all day long, in between making change for parking tokens. I'm willing to park cars at an embassy in the Middle East. All of these jobs would be a piece of cake compared to parenting.

Since I couldn't find the desk marked "Resign Here," I marched into my husband's office and said, "I quit. I don't want to be the stay-at-home parent anymore. In fact, I'm not sure I want to be a parent anymore at all. Maybe I could be a fond aunt or a godmother or something along those lines. I'd enjoy that, I think.

"I'm sick of the endless hours. I've had it with being an unappreciated short-order cook. I'm bored to death trying to come up with new punishments for people who throw their clothes on the floor six inches away from the conveniently located laundry hamper. I'm tired of entertaining, feeding, clothing, and chauffeuring my own and other people's children.

"I don't want to pay a small fortune to see mediocre kids' movies any more. I don't care how good the animation is. I don't want to hear the sounds of Nickelodeon, the Disney Channel, or ESPN Sports Center blaring from the television at all hours of the day and night. I want to control the stereo system in my own car. I want to hear songs with a melody I can hum and lyrics I can understand the words to again.

"I've had it with sacrificing my social life, my career goals, every second of free time, and every penny I own or borrow to indulge the iPod fantasies of the ungrateful wretches I gave birth to.

"I don't want to cajole anyone into doing his or her homework or practicing the piano ever again. I don't want to go to three stores to find blue jeans that are 'destroyed' already, cost more than my wedding dress, and then, instead of being the object of grateful appreciation, have to fight with my child to make sure they're pulled up far enough to hide his boxer shorts or make sure my daughter's belly button isn't on display.

"I don't want to wash other people's underwear anymore. I don't want to fold it or deliver it to my children's bedrooms and then beg them to take on the arduous task of opening the bureau drawers to put their clean, pressed clothes away. I don't want to discover the next morning that the neatly folded and meticulously ironed clothes were shoved willy-nilly into drawers so that they look like wadded-up towels used to wash the car.

"Kids are too much of a long-term investment. The delayed gratification of rearing kind and responsible adult citizens sounds good in theory, but the adult product is so far in the nebulous future it might as well be the pot of gold at the end of the rainbow. I don't even know where the rainbow is. We saw one in the ballpark once, but I don't know what happened to it.

"I just realized our kids are not even going to remember all the birthday parties, vacation trips, long summer days, and sacrifices of time, money, and attention we made for them when they were little. They're only going to remember a few incidents from childhood. They'll probably remember the times I yelled at them for forgetting their science books and not hanging up their bath towels and forget all about the nights I stayed up until midnight to make sure their baseball uniforms were clean for the next night's game.

"Do you realize that almost every child-rearing stage we have suffered through doesn't even count for anything in their memories? They aren't going to remember any of this! How much do you remember before high school? Not much, I bet. I don't."

"You can't quit," my husband replied, looking at me over the top of his reading glasses, still seated in his desk chair and typing away on the computer, obviously unimpressed by my melodramatic plea for emancipation.

"It's like the military—you sign up, you're in. You can't change your mind. Once the pregnancy test comes back positive, you're locked in for a lifetime. You can be removed for cause, of course . . ." he went on, an attorney and judge, waxing eloquently in a little legal speculation.

"Parental rights can be terminated, as you know. Courts do that all the time, but you're not really doing a bad enough parenting job for that," he finished up, with a hard look and a count-your-blessings glance at my poor-me, spread-eagle, prostrate position on the sofa.

"You don't understand," I continued. "I can't do it anymore. I'm over-educated for the job. I'm completely unappreciated. Oprah and Dr. Phil would say I'm in an abusive situation. I had no idea that after the actual labor and delivery—I note you didn't have much to do with that little party, either—the job of child-rearing itself would be such hard manual labor, akin to work in the local rock quarry. I had no idea it would involve word problems and mind reading when I signed on.

"I'm a: short-order cook, a hospital orderly, a laundress, a tutor, a chauffer, a coach, a courier, a shopper, a fashion consultant, a counselor, a cruise director, and, apparently, the stiffest disciplinarian since Attila the Hun and the only parent in America who cares whether or not the movie is rated PG or PG-13 or if a party has adult chaperones or not. The people I am slaving away for don't appreciate me. About half the time, they don't even *like* me. That really hurts my feelings. How can they not like me?

"They're actually ashamed of me and would, frankly, be quite content if I didn't open my mouth in front of their friends. As long as I agree to finance, chaperone, drive, and coordinate their vitally important social lives, our children would prefer that I be an invisible, hardworking house elf right out of the *Harry Potter* books.

"What well-educated, twenty-first-century woman would want this job? It's a trick! You start out with this sweet-smelling baby who loves you better than anyone on earth, and then they grow up to be . . . teenagers! It's such a *shock*.

"I haven't a dime to call my own. If I have to attend a funeral, I pay a baby-sitter ten dollars an hour to do the job I do for free, day in and day out. There are no vacation days. No sick days. I'm unpopular with the masses, always the bad cop and never the hero. I'm isolated from other adults like a member of a seventeenth-century penal colony. I can't even make a dentist appointment without checking four other people's schedules. This job stinks!"

"Well, yes, I thought you knew," my husband had the audacity to say to me *out loud*. This is a man who escapes every day for hours on end to the adult working world where people praise him for his work and where people not only do not have to make other people's meals but actually go out to lunch and peruse the menu in places that don't serve chicken fingers and macaroni and cheese.

This is the man who regularly comes home to a restocked pantry, household crises weathered, dinner prepared (well, sometimes), clothes miraculously clean and folded, and homework completed or in the process of being completed. He is routinely greeted like MacArthur returning to the Philippine Islands by children anxious to file human-rights allegations against the dictator left in charge of the home front all day.

"Bad day, huh? What do you want to do about it?" my husband asks. "Do you want me to stay home for a while?"

"You know perfectly well you can't do this job to my satisfaction. Neither can anyone else. That's why I signed on for the tour. Most of the time, it's worth it. Anyway, we can't live on my salary, and although it might be better for me personally to go back to work, it wouldn't do these ungrateful beasts we live with any good at all. They need twenty-four-hour policing. It takes years to learn the ropes. You wouldn't survive a week. These teenagers would walk all over you. It'd be like taking candy from a baby."

"What can I do for you?" he asked, a man obviously sympathetic and fearful that his chief executive officer is about to go AWOL in the middle of a shooting war with no regard for the consequences that would, undoubtedly, reek havoc in his own well-ordered life.

"Let's discuss perks," I suggest.

"Fine," my husband is quick to agree. "What can I do?"

"I'm going to need a glass of wine. And chocolate. LOTS of chocolate," I say.

"Do you want simple, heartfelt, conscience-stricken remorseful apologies from the children in person, or are we talking typed essays on 'What My Mother Does for Me' by morning?" he asks.

"I'm going to take a bubble bath and consider my employment options," I told him. "I suggest you go downstairs and have a heart-to-heart chat with those children who want to continue living here. Tell them I could make a small fortune as a professional nanny. This family certainly could not afford me. Tell them I'm looking into my options, and see how they like the idea of getting dropped off after breakfast and picked up in time for supper."

"That's pretty harsh," my husband said.

"Yeah, well, it's a tough world," I told him.

Telephone Manners

WHAT IN THE WORLD HAS HAPPENED TO OUR TELE-
phone manners? Am I the only mother insisting
that my children display polite telephone manners? Of course, I realize that my children don't
always use the nice telephone manners I have
explained to them meticulously at least a thousand times, but I certainly fuss at them when I
find out about it! Is there someone out there telling children—and adults, for that matter—that
basic rules of etiquette are no longer required in
our society? If so, that person should be rounded up and forced to write wedding thank-you
notes.

I am especially ashamed to report incidents of poor telephone manners in the South
since I consider our little corner of the world to
be one of the last bastions of decorum. We may
not be successful at coercing our children into
using good manners all the time, but down here,
Southern mamas are still trying.

What happened to the courtesy of callers identifying themselves before asking to speak to someone? I am astounded that civilized members of my community call and say, "Is —— there?" with no additional qualifying words of explanation. Children are the worst about it, but I also have adults who call and ask to speak to someone in my household without identifying themselves.

If that person is in residence, I have resorted to replying, "Yes." Full stop. I hope I am making the point that just because someone is home does not mean that he or she is taking telephone calls or accepting calls from this particular caller. Perhaps it is dinnertime. Maybe the child is doing homework and can't come to the telephone. Perhaps the family has company. Maybe, just maybe, the kid is in the bathtub! Surely, we have not reached such a low point in our civility with one another that I am expected to reveal that piece of personal information to an anonymous caller! Should I say, "He'll be with you in a minute. He's got one leg all soaped up, and he's about to start on the other one"? I don't doubt for a second that if I said so-and-so is "indisposed," I'd have to define indisposed.

This whole discussion is making me tired.

Thanks to Caller ID, we don't have to be victimized by every fund-raiser, pollster, or salesperson out there, but even among friends, it is nice to know who is calling. Sometimes, we all need a few moments to collect our wits or gird our loins before talking to the bishop or the school principal.

"Hello. This is ——. May [since obviously you *can*, or you wouldn't be on the horn] I please [a nice touch] speak to ——?" is the minimum standard. I prefer that the caller acknowledge the gracious person who has agreeably troubled him or herself to answer the phone. I think a few seconds of idle chitchat is a fair expectation, but if this is a real emergency, and someone is likely to die on the operating table unless you put so-and-so on the phone immediately, then a simple identification will do.

Teenagers have found a way around all the worrisome good-manners details, of course. In order to avoid all contact with odious adults entirely, they simply call each other on their cell phones, a thousand times an hour. The conversation is scintillating. It goes something like this:

"Hey, wuz up?"

"Nothin'. Wuz up wit you?"

"I'm bored. Wanna do somethin'?"

"Yeah. What?"

"I don't know. What do you want to do?"

This skillful repartee continues along those lines for hours on end. Teenagers call each other on cell phones while sitting on a couch in a home equipped with the full services provided by household landlines. In this way, teenagers are able to avoid those pesky adult middlemen or women altogether. It's a pretty clever plan when you think about it.

Aha. Not at my house. I ask all teenagers to check their cell phones at the door. Like a bouncer, I ask them to leave those suckers on the mantel on their way into my house. Some evenings, it looks like the entire contents of an electronic store have been thrown on my mantel. Teenagers squeal in protest over this rule. From their reactions, you'd think I'd asked them to remove their prosthetic legs or hearing aids to gain entry to my house. I'm not too sympathetic. Since I am quite certain their parents know where they are, and our telephone number is listed in the directory, I feel confident they can be located in the wilds of our suburban home if their presence is urgently needed.

Leaving those phones on the mantel also cuts down on all the emergency gossip teenagers feel they must discuss late at night and in the wee morning hours when adults who need their beauty rest are snoring away. My, oh, my . . . if some of those mamas knew their daughters were calling my sons at midnight, I know some heads would roll!

It seems such a long time ago when I urged my young children to talk to their grandparents on the telephone and explained, over and over again, that a nod didn't mean a thing to the person on the other end of the phone. Now that I think about it, I don't know why I ever encouraged my children to pick up the wretched telephone. I could have saved myself a whole lot of bother if they were still using tin cans and a string.

To Be Missed

WHEN MY OLDEST CHILD FIRST WENT TO SCHOOL, HIS younger brother would sit on the sidewalk and sob. There wasn't much I could do to comfort him because he didn't miss me; he missed his brother's presence all day long. All along our walk to school, he would beg his brother not to leave him.

"Please don't go," he'd plead. "I'll miss you too much."

No matter how much reassurance I offered, it was months before my younger son could tell his brother to have a good day without sounding heartbroken. It was a hard time. This is the same child who came into my bedroom the first time his older brother spent the night away from home and told me, "I can't sleep without my brother's breathin'."

A few years later, my younger son began school, and we went through the same trauma when my daughter was the one left behind. I'd remind my son, "Hug your sister goodbye;

remember how hard it was when your brother left you behind?" My daughter would turn her face away, refusing to acknowledge the fact that her brother was leaving her behind for the day.

No question about it. My husband and I always say our children may get fed up with us one day and plot our demise, but they'd have no trouble working together to hide the bodies. They love each other. Since sibling relationships are the longest of our lives, I think that's a good thing, but I can tell you I feel a bit nervous sometimes when I see all three of their little heads huddled together after one of them has been reprimanded. I just *know* they're talking about me.

Recently, on our way to the ballpark, my daughter complained bitterly and loudly about being the one who is always left behind, and I was interested to hear my middle child explain the facts of life to her.

"Let me tell you something," he said. (This should be interesting, I thought, since I never know what is going to come out of my middle child's mouth.)

"Are you going to miss me while I'm gone?" he asked her.

"*Yes!*" she answered, emphatically. "I want you to stay with me!"

"Sure you'll miss me," he said, his chest swelling visibly with pride. "It's nice to be missed. That means somebody loves you. How'd you like it if nobody missed you? You'd be lonely."

Well said, I thought.

Things Children Do That Make Me Want to Quit My Mommy Job

They throw their dirty clothes on the bathroom floor right next to—but not actually *inside*—the laundry hamper.

They wait until we're on the way out the front door to leave for school to tell me they are supposed to bring snacks, a new notebook, an exotic plant, or ten dollars in quarters to school that day.

They pretend to be suddenly deaf when I ask them to do something while they are watching television or when I tell them it's time for bed.

They throw away huge wads of chewed bubblegum—unwrapped—so that I have to reach in their bedroom garbage cans with my bare hands to pry it off the side.

They regularly leave long strands of toothpaste in their bathroom sinks until it dries to the consistency of bathroom calk in order to avoid the onerous task of simply washing the sink out after brushing their teeth.

They drop shampoo bottles in the shower and then leave them to empty drop by drop down the drain.

They use three clean towels during every hour-long shower extravaganza and then toss them carelessly across freshly made beds and antique furnishings as if they are Elvis and crowds of fans are screaming for their still-wet towels.

They drink the last few ounces of orange juice or milk and put the empty cartons back in the refrigerator.

They bitterly complain about regular haircuts as if their heads are being shaved for brain surgery or boot camp.

They ask for money to replace the money I gave them fifteen minutes earlier that has inexplicably disappeared.

They never voluntarily or spontaneously wash their hands.

They claim that there isn't anything to eat after I unload $350 worth of groceries.

They tell me they're bored when the entire contents of a toy store, an electronics store, and a sporting goods store line the walls of their bedrooms.

They roll their eyes at me when I talk about good manners.

They stuff freshly washed, recently ironed clothes into their drawers like wadded-up cleaning rags.

They throw trash into garbage cans across the room like a game-winning buzzer shot in basketball, miss, and then fail to get the rebound or make a lay-up.

They argue incessantly about rules they cannot change—like why they are the only kids in the Southeast with a bedtime, why they have to check the rating of the movie everyone else is allowed to see, and why they can't have Coke to drink with supper.

They can remember the batting average of every pitcher in the major leagues, but they cannot remember to open their napkins and place them in their laps even though they've been told to do so at least once a day for their entire lives.

They stand in the middle of the kitchen and open a bottled water to drink.

They play outside in their socks.

My Other Jobs

Special Treatment

IF YOU THINK WRITING BOOKS FOR A LIVING GETS ME off the hook when it comes to laundry duty, then you better think again. I'm still the washerwoman, and my personal nemesis is still the mountain of dirty clothes piled at the bottom of the basement stairs every morning. To put it mildly, laundry duty is one of my least favorite responsibilities, but since I am extremely fond of clean clothes, I don't see any way to avoid it.

Since I'm not overly thrilled to sort laundry in the first place, there are few things I despise more than laundry items with tags requesting special treatment. We don't dole out special treatment around here unless it's someone's birthday or someone has spiked a high fever. We are certainly not inclined to pamper mass-produced clothing items.

I am astounded that there is anyone in the world who buys lingerie that requires dry-cleaning. I know there must be someone out there willing to do so because (in my obsessive laundry-label reading while shopping) I have seen with my own two eyes such articles for sale. I don't mind admitting I would really be interested in meeting a person who has knowingly bought such a garment for lounging. (If it was just a poor slob of a husband trying to buy his wife a nightgown for Valentine's Day who didn't have the sense to check the label, then I don't think we should hold it against him.) I have a few things to say to people who have so much money they can afford to have their pajamas dry-cleaned. I've got a long list of charities where that money will do a whole lot more good than having their boxer shorts professionally pressed. As far as I can tell, this is the easiest test I have ever seen to identify people who have more money than sense. Maybe it should be a question members of the press ask candidates for public office. "Do you now, or have you ever had your pajamas dry-cleaned?" If the answer is yes, we don't need to know any more. People shouldn't handle taxpayer money if they've paid to dry-clean their underwear. Period.

Even for those of us who are truly gifted at stain removal (one of my few vanities, I admit it), there are so many laundry disasters just waiting to happen that you have to wonder about people who add needlessly to an endless chore. No woman who washes three loads a day, minimum, would ever intentionally create more laundry for herself or anyone else. I assure you that I have better things to do with my time. Even if I didn't have anything better to do, I'd make something up, and it wouldn't have anything to do with matching socks. I feel I am overqualified for any job the average preschooler could perform while watching *Sesame Street*.

Some of the most puzzling, just-asking-for-it laundry chores I've encountered in my life may have dirtied your life upon occasion, as well. My all-time worst cleaning list includes:

1) White baseball pants. I've written about this before, but I just can't seem to get it out of my system. I'm still whining about it. Why in the world would these be designed in white? To make matters worse, we actually teach and encourage kids to slide in the dirt and mud. I assume professional baseball players have a service that washes their pants for a fee, but around here, I'm the only game in town, and the white pants are just asking for it, in my opinion. The only saving grace is that with white, you can bleach until the cows

come home, no holds barred. (Did you know "hold" is a command knights used in jousting tournaments? It was kind of like a time-out. I just read that in a children's knight tale. I found it interesting, and I thought you might, too.)

2) Wall-to-wall carpet. Any way you look at it, carpet is a bad idea. When we went from dirt floors to wood floors, that made sense. Wood floors were, obviously, much easier to keep clean, and spilled milk did not result in a muddy dining room. The addition of handmade rugs was another plus. Rugs add color, warmth, and comfort for the toes. Dirt, spills, and stains don't show on fine Persian rugs. Take those rugs out and beat them every once in while, and you're in good shape. (I cheat and vacuum regularly. What do I care if those rugs don't make it to another generation? I'll be dead then.) Carpet is a whole different story. It's a terrible premise. I don't know what people were thinking. It's as if we each picked out fabric and glued it to the floor to walk on—on purpose. Of course, it gets filthy. That's what happens when you walk on cloth with your shoes on. You can't jerk it up and wash it. Pet stains, spills, dirty tennis shoes—there's no way to keep it stain-free, even if you buy an arsenal of rug-cleaning products, like I do. The carpet craze is a national hoax on the scale of bottled water.

3) Foreign Objects. Bubblegum. Candy. Pollen. There is just no end to the world of foreign bodies that can become your worst laundry nightmare. A seemingly innocent brown M&M can become a ground-in polka dot on your damask sofa for all time.

4) Bodily fluids. In order to maintain a self-imposed minimum standard of good manners, I cannot go into too much detail in this section, but suffice it to say that mothers who do laundry must have strong constitutions (and a controlled gag reflex) to treat assorted stains due to bloody knees, snotty noses, and throw-up viruses. If you are a parent, use your imagination here. Disgusting, isn't it?

5) Treasures. For some reason that is a complete mystery to those of us without a *Y* chromosome, boys put every treasure they encounter during their day's ramblings into their pockets. They do not, however, remember to remove those items from their pockets to throw them away. When sorting laundry, I search each pocket thoroughly and cautiously in my boys' pants because I have learned

the hard way what five chocolate candy Kisses can do to a load of whites as well as how much damage a fist-full of rusty screws can do to a washing machine. What I cannot abide are the LIVE (or recently expired) animals I have found in my children's pockets. Over the years, I have turned out: an assortment of worms, wriggling and non-wriggling; locust shells; snails; slugs; bird feathers; eggshells (who knows what species); and other natural artifacts as if my children have been hired to stock the local natural-science museum.

Writing is a Real Job

MY PRIMARY JOB IS REARING THREE CHILDREN. I AGREE with Jackie Kennedy Onassis that if I screw that up, nothing else I do will matter very much. Like most women I know, however, I have about fifteen other jobs in addition to that one. I'm also a chauffer, a courier, a short-order cook, a social secretary, a laundress—you've heard the list before.

Writing is a fun job, but I have to tell you that making time for writing falls way down on my priority list. The stars have to be perfectly aligned. No one in my house can be running a fever. I'm about fourth in line for computer time—right behind my second grader's book-report project. I share our home office with my husband, so he has to clear out. Everyone in my household has to have clean underwear for the next day, or, at the very least, there has to be a load in the dryer. In other words, writing time is scarce. It doesn't just happen. I have to sort of muscle it into the day and be prepared to weather the consequences of statements like, "I don't know what we're having for dinner. You're on your own. I'm writing." I tell you right now that you can't say that kind of thing too often, no matter how gutsy you are. It's just inviting a full-scale mutiny. In my experience, it's best to keep the natives well fed.

Since writing is about my third or fourth most important job, right behind laundry, I have to write when I have time, regardless of distractions, and I am always under a time constraint. I find it hard to be witty in a forty-five minute block of time. Often, when I have time to write, I find I have nothing whatsoever to say. On the other hand, when I'm multitasking like an astronaut strapped in a space shuttle, I find myself scrambling for paper and a pen to jot down four or five pages of really good stuff. I've begun carrying around small, blank notebooks. It saves me from having to decipher my horrible handwriting from the backs of bank deposit slips and cocktail napkins.

When someone asks me what I do all day, it's socially accept-able for me to say, "I'm a mom," or "I'm a teacher," but if I say, sheepishly, "I'm a writer," it sounds like I think I'm Miss Eudora Welty come back to life or something. Believe me; I'm under no such delusions of grandeur. Worse, friends act like I'm going to check every thank-you note they write me for grammar mistakes. I'll notice those mistakes, sure, but I won't point them out. I have nice manners!

About once a year, I find a small error in spelling, grammar, syntax, or some other strange idiom of our language in a piece that has made it all the way to the printer without being spotted. By then, it's too late to correct it, of course, and I have to begin the live-with-it phase. My children often witness my embarrassment when I discover an overlooked mistake when it is too late to revise it. They try to comfort me.

"Everybody makes mistakes, Mom," they say.

"I know, I *know*," I reply.

Because I taught them that premise, I can hardly throw myself under a train at the thought of the occasional error, as appealing as that might be. To tell the truth, I've had about all the humility les-sons I can stand.

You better believe I diligently proofread every piece many

times, but, inevitably, I occasionally miss something that later causes me private remorse, public humiliation, and generally serves to delight former writing students who read the published piece and then email me to gloat over my editing transgressions. Believe me, when writers make a mistake in print, we get 350 emails gleefully pointing out the error. We're the last people in the world to gloat over mistakes made by other people.

I am not by nature a careless person. In fact, I regularly check dictionaries, handbooks, and the Internet when faced with thorny writing dilemmas. Nor am I an arrogant writer. I own up freely to egregious errors of ignorance and apologize profusely for careless mistakes. On a related note, I'd like to go on record stating that I find computer self-checks only marginally helpful; I've had some heated debates with my computer over a few choice colloquial-isms. It's not easy to argue with a computer—inflexible, horrid little machines. No soul and no sense of humor, computers, that's the whole problem, as I see it. Unfortunately, I cannot imagine making it through a single day of writing without my computer. As you may have gathered, I have a complicated love-hate relationship with my laptop.

If you are a writer, this will probably all sound familiar to you. If you're not, then you just thank your lucky stars you have a regu-lar job that doesn't embarrass you in public. No sane person would choose to make a living as a writer. It's a handicap you're born with like bushy eyebrows. It would be easier to do almost anything else, and most writers end up writing by default after fighting the urge for their entire lives. This has certainly been true for me.

At its best, writing is sporadic work, rarely profitable, and spi-rals between the sublime and self-indulgent drivel. Unfortunately, it is as necessary to some of us as breathing in and out. Fish gotta swim. Birds gotta fly. Writers gotta write.

Sometimes I wish God had made me the fish or the bird.

Career Opportunities

I HAVE A THEORY THAT EACH ONE OF US IS IDEALLY suited to a job in our society. This doesn't mean, of course, that we all find that job or we are actually hired to do it. In America, we are almost never born to it. This explains why I am not queen of anything. Often, we are not educated or trained to the appropriate degree to qualify for the dream job. Finally and most obviously, real life often has a habit of getting in the way of our vocational dreams. Surely, somewhere in the sultry South there is someone who longs to win the Iditarod dog sled race and someone who fantasizes about growing up to be a Samurai warrior. Unfortunately, there aren't many opportunities for those career goals to flourish down here.

It is also a sad truth that when we are offered made-in-heaven choice positions, we are gifted at finding ways to sabotage ourselves. We frequently squander the opportunities, burn the bridges, and puncture the golden parachutes behind us. I believe Southerners, in particular, have raised the art of unemployment to a level of cultural hubris.

I recognize that there are exceptions to my everyone-is-employable theory. You get weird genetic mutations in every species. However, I believe that if we are creative and open-minded, and if we are trying to employ a non-brain-damaged individual with an ounce of common sense and a speck of self-respect and personal initiative, we can find him or her a job. If we can just discover each person's talent, there is a job for even the most obnoxious, mouth-breathing, socially inept person with the intelligence quotient of a potted fern.

I admit I have been accused of seeing the glass not only half-full but running over with potential in the middle of a drought, but I think I'm on to something. There's no point in rolling your eyes at me. This is my story, and I'm sticking to it.

When I worked as a college teacher, I can't tell you how many times I ran into a problem where either the parent or the student was just determined on one course of study—regardless of the student's natural inclination, talent, physical or mental abilities.

I remember one woman who was determined to work in broadcast journalism. She seemed oblivious to the fact that her voice was completely atonal—she had no more vocal variety in her request to pass the salt than when she warned you a pit bull was about to bite you on the behind.

Another one of my students was gifted artistically, but her father was determined she was going to law school. I tried unsuccessfully to tactfully advise her to major in her academic gifts. Finally, when her abysmal first-term grades came in, I got her father on board by asking him, "Does the world really need another angry attorney?"

One student I knew was uninterested in his coursework, immature, and not the best candidate for hanging in there for the four-year degree. His parents took his one interest, golf, and found a special program that got him a college degree and a future job selling golf carts and playing golf for a living without having to make the cut on the professional touring circuit. I wanted to kiss those parents right on the mouth.

One of my favorite career stories (which also supports my job theory, naturally) features a mentally disabled man who sorts tickets at community sporting events. He doesn't count them. He doesn't add up the proceeds. He doesn't record the results. He sorts the tickets by color into different piles. That's his job. He is superb at it, and it gives purpose, dignity, and meaning to his life. A little warning: he takes his sorting job seriously, and woe unto you if you get in his way. He's not exactly flexible regarding his professional calling.

Unfortunately, the converse of my job theory is also true. There are jobs from which some people should be barred—regardless of talent, mental ability, or cleverness—merely because their own personality quirks make them a danger to themselves and others. Some people can't assume authoritarian roles. These people cannot handle the pressures associated with any type of uniform, badge, or gun. Millions of people handle such roles with ease, but there is one personality type that goes haywire when awarded minor trappings of power. For those of you who know *The Andy Griffith Show*, this phenomenon can be summed up with the character of Barney Fife. Remember how Barney was allowed to carry a gun, but he had to keep the bullet in his pocket? That just turned out to be the safest thing for everyone.

We all know people like that. Often, they have military-style, low-pile haircuts even though they never actually served in the military. You may have encountered a library security officer who threatened to beat gum-smacking library patrons into submission, or you may have run into a movie usher who shined his flashlight directly into your eyes to force you to confess whether or not you had your feet propped up on the seat in front of you. Maybe you've crossed paths with a deputy sheriff, sporting mirror sunglasses and an earpiece, who privately viewed himself as a member of the presidential security detail. Somewhere in their DNA, these people have some tiny chromosomal flaw that makes them abuse any type of authority they have over others, a bit too much of the ambition gene putting them right up there with knife-wielding Roman senators in the last days of March.

There's a simple antidote for parking attendants and others who get a little too badge-happy. They should avoid jobs offering power-status playthings—guns, uniforms, night sticks, etc.—in the same way alcoholics avoid working as bartenders. Simple. If you know your strengths and weaknesses, you can avoid potential minefields.

I don't deny that some people are hard to place. At a mother's insistence, I once sent a lazy, undisciplined, mushroom-IQ-bearing student to the campus career-services counselor to take a computer-based talent survey to find unexplored opportunities for him. His mom was convinced that *all* of her son's professors were missing his academic worth.

You know what that survey suggested would be a good match for that boy?

Shepherding. I'm not kidding. I wish I could say I made that up, but I didn't. I can tell you it made me pretty curious about what the rest of the computer database contained as career options for American college students. What else might we find? Pimping?

Now. Do you think I gave up on that lazy, good-for-nothing, frustrating troll of boy? No, I did not. I'll have you know we folded that shepherding talent right into horticulture. I figured if he can take care of sheep, then he can take care of a bunch of daffodil bulbs, right? Well, okay, he now mows lawns for a living, but that's a perfectly respectable profession. He's happy. He's productive. He insists on being paid in cash, so he might not be doing society any great tax-paying service, but he's not sucking up to our tax base like an amoebic parasite either.

I consider that a success story. I'm even willing to go out on a limb and predict there's an even-money chance he'll show up to mow my lawn next week.

The Business License

THIS MAY COME AS A SURPRISE TO YOU. IT CERTAINLY surprised me. Today's SWAG life lesson is: The easiest thing about publishing a book is writing it. That's the fun part. Words bubble up like cheap shampoo when I'm on a roll, and, lucky for me, the SWAGs in my life provide me with plenty of humorous material, some I can actually write about without getting sued. More often than not, I feel like a stenographer, someone who pays close attention to what's happening around me and jots down the highlights—with a little hyperbole, of course. We Southerners know how to tell a story.

The hard part about writing a book is the pesky business details that I would much rather ignore. Unfortunately, as we all know, inattention to the small details of business—taxes and licenses, for example—has led to extended vacations in the state penitentiary. You all know how I feel about those unflattering orange jumpsuits.

While it is undeniably true that I am bored to death by the business side of a book's publication, I have a well-developed fear of being separated from the luxuries I consider life sustaining—things like bubble baths, Swiss chocolate, and crushed ice on demand. I have pressing engagements that do not allow for time spent in handcuffs. In other words, I pay attention to my accountant, and he's trained me to hold on to receipts like a squirrel hoarding nuts for the winter.

Usually, when writers autograph books for readers, their appearances are hosted by bookstores that stock and sell their books. It's a win/win situation. The bookstore provides authors with a place for people to buy the book and meet the writer. In return, authors bring customers into the bookstore. (Bookstores, incidentally, make much more money on each book than writers do.) It's a simple capitalist transaction.

Occasionally, however, writers like me can't resist the temptation and agree to speak to fun groups of women who then want to buy the book on the spot, even if it's ten o'clock at night. On a Sunday. On a desert island. In the middle of a hurricane. Readers aren't remotely concerned about who gets the sales tax. They aren't interested in excuses about how impossible it is for the author of the book to schlep books onto an airplane, into a taxi, into an elevator, up to a hotel room, across a pedestrian-only bridge, and five miles down to a beach for a picturesque-conference or resort-vacation book signing somewhere off the coast of Georgia. Book lovers don't care if Al-Qaeda handles the book sales. If they enjoyed hearing the author's presentation, they want to take the book home with them to read right then.

Makes sense, doesn't it? Well, of course. Except for one thing. If there isn't a bookstore on site (with those lovely bookstore employees who know all about how the paperwork is supposed to be filled out), then it's up to the author to figure the minutia out to the satisfaction of Uncle Sam.

Let me tell you right now that most writers are not too gifted at that sort of thing. There are chimpanzees with better mental math skills than I have. I am a woman who routinely makes my children figure out the tip in a restaurant. I'm not even embarrassed about it. I made *A*s is my math classes. I didn't really understand it, but I made *A*s. However, that was a long time ago. I'm not doing math anymore. I'm over it. That's why God made calculators.

Tax forms make me tired and slightly anxious, like I'm probably going to leave out something important and get deported or lose my right to vote or something. The sight of a bunch of rigid, empty blanks irritates me. What if I need more room? I don't like my words to be constrained by someone else's limited fill-in-the-blank space. I'm more of an essay-question girl. Whenever there is a fill-in-the-blank, yes-or-no question, I always have doubts. The older I get, the more gray area I see in the world.

Let me give you one likely hypothetical problem. What am I supposed to do when a customer needs to make an emergency book purchase for her mother-in-law? What if this customer forgot to buy her mother-in-law a birthday gift, and she is meeting her for lunch in forty-five minutes, and we all agree my book will be perfect for the old dragon, but, unfortunately, the customer locked her purse in the car and can't get the spare key until her husband comes home from a business trip tomorrow night? I deal with Southern women all the time, and I'm telling you that this is a likely scenario. I don't know about you, but I'm not about to get in the middle of a mother-in-law birthday situation. I have more sense than that. I assure you that having an audience comprised mostly of Southern women presents its own unique set of problems.

After my book tour was over, a number of readers asked me if I would be their guest speaker for some event they were hosting. (Of course for a fee; I'm not doing this just for fun, you know. The fun is just a perk.) I began to research how one goes about selling books at an event for which one is, essentially, the live entertainment. Believe me; a reading is not that different from juggling, telling jokes, or singing at a wedding. Most audiences are looking for a little fun.

Pretty soon, I started thinking about business licenses. For me, thinking about something is just a heartbeat away from worrying about it. I began worrying about business licenses right on cue late one night after everyone I know who can answer questions about business licenses is in bed asleep.

It took me a while, but I finally faced up to reality. I realized that I would have to buy a business license. It was a task way out of my comfort zone, so I had to work up the nerve, and I was feeling rather pleased with myself one morning as I set off for the courthouse. I felt proud to be part of interstate commerce, glad to do my civic duty, happy to live up to my tax-paying responsibilities and support the community I love—that sort of dreamy drivel. It didn't take long before my little good-citizen fantasy ran smack into civil-service reality.

Since I am a law-abiding, mind-numbingly responsible citizen, when I got to the front of the courthouse line, the first thing I asked is if I do, indeed, need a business license to sell my own stinkin' book.

"Oh, yes, ma'am, of course, you need a business license," was the immediate response to my half-hearted query. I immediately felt overwhelmed and out of my depth, due to my lack of business savvy and keen entrepreneurial drive, as if someone might, at any moment, quiz me on my multiplication tables or how to convert Fahrenheit degrees to Celsius.

All in all, I found the experience to be exhausting and slightly humiliating. In a comments box I found nailed to the courthouse wall, I suggested individually wrapped chocolates for customers who had successfully reached the front of the line. Lord knows it would have perked me up.

All the while, my youngest child was hanging on to my skirt and asking me approximately a hundred questions per minute, things like:

"Why does that lady have an earring in her belly button?"

"Do you want to hear what is on my Christmas list?"

"Why are there naked angels on the walls? Are they getting ready to take a bath?"

"Is that our neighbor's picture on the wall? What does FBI mean?"

Needless to say, it was hard for me to gather my thoughts in a professional manner. My blood pressure was sky high when the city clerk informed me, with a smirk on her face that would have gotten her a week of no television at my house, that I would not be dragged off to the pokey if I did not buy the business license in the next five minutes. I was free, she said, to take the paperwork home and study it at my leisure.

"What leisure?" I muttered in a petty, bad-tempered way I'm not proud of in retrospect.

Quickly glancing over the form, I was shocked to discover I would first have to pay a seventy-five dollar application fee. Since I was not applying for graduate school in a foreign country or to open a topless bar, I thought that was a little steep.

Second, I was informed that there was no guarantee I would actually receive the business license itself at all. This was merely an expensive preliminary step. I would then be required to take the original business license application, along with seven copies; a survey of my house; the names and addresses of my neighbors; and several other seemingly irrelevant and mystifying documents I hadn't seen outside of a safety-deposit box in the last fifteen or so years to a municipal building located somewhere in East Jerusalem.

"Are you kidding me?" I asked the clerk. "I'm not about to open a Wal-mart, you know. We're talking about selling a few books after I give a speech to a book club."

"Form's the same for everyone," she said, popping her gum in my face. "We don't play favorites," she added, with pursed lips and a pious tone, like I was secretly trying to buy a business license to harvest human organs for sale on eBay.

Because I am the mother of three children, I am accustomed to life's little curve balls, seemingly insurmountable obstacles, and constant small frustrations, so I took a deep breath, counted to ten, and resolved to hold on to my temper.

Flinging open the door to city hall, I was not the least bit surprised to discover it was still pouring rain outside, and someone had—unintentionally, I am sure—swiped my umbrella where I had thoughtfully left it dripping by the door.

"Somebody stole my princess umbrella, Mommy!" my daughter fairly squealed.

"Don't worry about it, sweetie," I replied. "We've got bigger fish to fry today."

"We're having fish?" my daughter asked, completely distracted. My metaphors are unappreciated in my own household.

I guess I don't need to tell you I was already miffed as I drove, dripping wet, to the copy store and then to the far-flung municipal offices to fulfill my civic duty.

The next round of watching my tax dollars at work involved

being educated by a bored and rather sickly (she sneezed on me twice) city employee about how this next step in my business-license process would work.

Obviously, it would be easier to move up the papal ladder to beautification, canonization, and sainthood than it would be to get an eight-and-a-half-by-eleven piece of paper permitting me to buy and sell books. Every mom-and-pop hot-dog stand in America has a business license. My manicurist successfully completed the business-license-purchase process. She keeps it thumb-tacked over her pink-nail-polish shelf.

Am I so different?

Next, I received the joyful news that I would have to appear in person before my city's zoning board to petition for a special exemption for my business license since I did not actually have an address for the premises-location line on the form. You see what I mean? Big problem: an empty blank on the form. Southern women are unique individuals. We're not fill-in-the-blank kind of women. Never have been. Never will be. End of discussion.

Well, obviously, I should have just made up an address. I could have put the address for the public library. No one would have noticed or cared, but I'm not hard-wired to lie, and it's a shame. I can't lie about an expired grocery-store coupon, even when it would come in real handy and not harm a fly.

Now, I ask you: Have you ever in your life heard of a writer having to appear before her zoning board to sell books at speaking events? I think not. I knew there was some mistake. I just couldn't figure out what to do about it. Maybe I'd started out in the wrong line. . . .

In addition, I was informed I had just missed the fifteen-day cutoff to appear on the current month's agenda and would have to hurry up and wait another month.

Naturally.

I made one last appeal for bureaucratic sanity: "Listen to me. This is not a business. This is just a couple of boxes of books that go with me to speaking events. I'm not a businesswoman! I could sink Microsoft if I worked there! I'm not even sure I'm coming out ahead after I pay for this business license. When the accountant figures it all out, I may be in big trouble!"

The courthouse clerk seemed totally unmoved by my Oscar-worthy plea for understanding. She spent the entire time I was pleading my case reading a list on the back of my book. (To buy a business license, you have to bring a sample of your business product. All I could think to do was to bring a copy of the book.) I suppose I should have been gratified by the fact that the clerk was laughing out loud. *I was not.*

A few days later, the city planted one of those yellow, plastic, public-hearing signs in my front yard. When I came wheeling into my driveway after picking up my children from school, there it was, big as life, stuck right in my lawn. As you can imagine, I was absolutely mortified.

For the next few weeks, I couldn't even sit on my own front porch swing without being questioned by neighbors about that sign. On Halloween night, I handed out apologetic explanations along with the candy to all my neighbors.

As a further humiliation, the city made me pay for certified letters to all my neighbors to notify them about potential sales. Several times each day, I explained to my sweet neighbor who has Alzheimer's disease that I was not planning to open a McDonald's or anything like that next-door to her house.

When the night of the zoning hearing finally arrived, I was past the nervous stage and just plain fed up. Clearly, this had all been one big misunderstanding. I didn't have time to worry too much beforehand because I couldn't find a baby-sitter, and I arrived just as the meeting was being called to order.

If you've never been to a zoning hearing, I have to say it is one of those first experiences in life that sticks in your memory. Like death, taxes, and sex, you can't really appreciate it fully until you experience it firsthand.

The contractors, engineers, and architects looked bored, but I was shocked at the formality of the proceedings. The zoning board members were seated on a raised dais draped in red, white, and blue bunting. Citizen petitioners were seated in chairs below the dais like school children in detention.

As soon as I found a seat, I was handed a typed agenda and

quickly found my name printed there with an assigned case number next to it like I was some sort of common jewelry thief.

As I waited for my case number to be called, I was painfully aware that I was the only person there without a buddy and wished, rather belatedly, that I had rounded up a few girlfriends for moral support. I also wished I had reapplied my lipstick and ironed the blouse I had been wearing since 6 AM.

All around me were elaborate posters and sleek presentations on easels. I had a yellow sticky note stuck to my purse to remind me to stop by the grocery store for milk on the way home and a copy of my book that I grabbed on the way out the door. Frankly, I didn't think my chances looked too promising.

Two-and-a-half hours later, I watched as the petitioner in front of me had her business license vetoed after she delivered an impassioned speech intoning our founding fathers, the American Way, her family's work ethic, and God's will. I don't think the zoning board would have been impressed if she had been Miss America holding an apple pie. They ruled on the letter of the law. She lost.

Finally, it was my turn. As I walked to the microphone, I had the feeling I was asking for the indulgence of some royal court rather than merely requesting permission to sell my own book. I was amazed that these men (every last one of them) volunteered their time for this committee. I would rather be beaten with a stick than serve on the zoning board, but I guess it's good someone is willing to do it since our zoning board does need to safeguard our neighborhoods from potentially dangerous writing entrepreneurs like me.

I took a novel approach in my presentation. I began by saying that book sales at non-bookstore venues would be rare. I admitted that the entirety of my business was contained in the bottom drawer of my dining-room sideboard, and I am only free to use the computer when everyone's homework is done, and I call a halt to the endless stream of instant messages to and from teenagers in my home.

I don't think the zoning board has a well-developed sense of humor. Nevertheless, I eventually got unanimous approval for my business license, and the board magnanimously allowed me to write the city yet another huge check. I'm not entirely sure the city did me a favor. I love to write books, but book sales are not really my thing. I tell you one thing—I don't want to hear one word of complaint about the price of this book. Believe me, a book is a bargain buy.

Ten Things About Writing

Five things I love about writing:

1) I love to make people laugh. This is one of the best feelings in the world. To distract someone for a few minutes from real life is my greatest writing accomplishment.

2) Money I make by writing allows me to replace things my children break around the house. I make enough here and there to keep up with the breakage and to occasionally splash out on something just for fun.

3) Writing keeps me sane. Writing is cheaper than therapy, which I certainly cannot afford. With all the athletic injuries, flu bugs, and orthodontic work around here, we don't have time for any medical frills that are not covered by insurance. Writing about a real-life experience and reducing it to a humorous interlude puts life in perspective for me, makes me jerk my priorities in line, and probably keeps me out of prison.

4) Writing books allows me to meet other women from all over the place who are just like me. It's incredibly reassuring. In addition, for someone like me who doesn't get out all that much, it's pretty darn interesting to hear about all the things other women get up to. I get a lot of good material that way.

5) Writing is the grownup version of tattling. When someone infuriates, irritates, or frustrates me, I can always write about the incident and get the same satisfaction I used to get as a child when I told on someone. Tattling is very cathartic. It's the nice way to get even. In fact, I think tattling is a highly underrated activity. A little tattling can go a long way toward solving a problem. It's good to tattle on bullies. Think about it. And even if a problem has no possible satisfactory resolution, once you've told your best friend all about it, you feel better anyway, don't you? I know I do.

Five things I hate about writing:

1) I rarely have time to write. I know writers have been whining about this forever, but it's still true. If you are the primary caretaker of three children, you know what I mean. There is no free time. I never finish my to-do list, so when I take time to write, I always feel guilty about the other tasks I'm neglecting. There are always other chores I should be doing that are not nearly as much fun as writing. Like the poor people Jesus said would always be with us, I always have permanent tasks on my to-do list: laundry, laundry, and more laundry; bathrooms that need to be cleaned before they become a health hazard; floors that must be mopped before someone slips on the squished English peas; errands that need to be run before strangers begin to notice we're out of deodorant at our house; and checking accounts that simply must be reconciled before I make another purchase over ten dollars. You know the list. Right this minute, there is enough hair on my daughter's bathroom floor to make a wig, and the fish tank is so dark and dirty in my son's bedroom you can't even see the fish anymore. I'm not sure they're even alive in there.

2) I don't have my own computer or office. My husband and I share a small office space at home. (Just try it. This is not an idea to promote marital harmony.) The whole family shares one computer that sits on a desk in that office. All this means I'm about fifth in line for computer time. My husband's job provides the health insurance, so I'm all for him using the home computer when he needs it. In addition, I'm a big fan of getting homework done ASAP, so, of course, I have to bow out when the kids need the computer for schoolwork. (However, when I catch them just sucking up time instant messaging their friends, I feel just fine about booting them off the computer so I can work.) I long for my own laptop, a computer that would not share space with kids' games and four other email accounts. On a hopeful note, my eight-year-old daughter is currently entered in a *Reading Rainbow* contest where first prize is a laptop. It's nationwide, but, hey, it could happen, right? As you can imagine, we're all unselfishly rooting for her to win.

3) When I do have time to write, and the calendar is miracu-

lously clear of dental appointments, baseball games, birthday parties, and cooking and cleaning duties, and I sit down to write for a few glorious hours of uninterrupted work, I find that I have nothing to say. Not a thing. I sharpen pencils, reorganize my paper clips, line stacks of to-do projects up neatly on the desk, and . . . sit there. It never fails. I always have something really good to jot down in the middle of the carpool pickup line at school or while I'm icing fifty cupcakes for the middle-school bake sale. I have never, not once, personally experienced a picturesque writing moment like the ones I see in scholarly magazines. You know the photographs I mean. The writer is posed at an antique desk in an outfit both casual and elegant. (A photograph of me in my casual clothes would make you think, "I bet she is just about to do some yard work.") In the glossy photographs, the writer always appears diligent, as if he or she is just about to type the final words of a prize-winning manuscript. Often, the writer has an editing pencil clenched loosely between his or her teeth. On the desk, a cup of premium-blend, aromatic coffee steams invitingly. That's nice for a magazine layout, but it has never worked that way for me. Ever. Not once. I don't even drink coffee, and our office is furnished with castoffs from the rest of the house, so the décor fairly screams yard sale.

    4) Writing does not always follow my plan. You know I like a plan. I am not a fly-by-the-seat-of-her-pants kind of gal. Unfortunately, I often sit down to write about one topic and end up writing about something entirely different. Much as it goes against my grain, I am forced to go where the writing takes me, so I am often piqued when I plan to write about a recent wedding reception, for example, and I end up with a chapter on the intricacies of a particular spinach quiche recipe. I just never know what's going to happen. You can imagine how upsetting this sort of thing is to my table-of-contents plans. I often have to rethink the whole thing.

    5) I feel responsible for other people's book ideas. When I sign books for people, they often tell me about their own book projects. I've heard some really interesting pitches. However, I'm a *writer*, not a *publisher*. There's not a thing I can do for those people except to wish them luck. Nevertheless, I feel I should be more helpful. Once a teacher, always a teacher, I believe.

The Suburban Wilderness

The Holly Tree

I'LL JUST BE UP FRONT ABOUT IT AND SAY THAT I'M
not really a yard work kind of person. I have
no intention of ever learning how to operate a
lawn mower because I might then be required
to use one. I have enough jobs around here.
I'm not looking to add anything else to my list.
I do, however, like to *dabble* in gardening. In
other words, I am quite content with a couple
of hours of yard work every season, and I like
to wear my cute gardening gloves and hat. The
only tools I'm interested in using are a small
trowel and pruning shears. Really, I just like to
loop a basket over my arm, gather up everything
in bloom, and take it inside to arrange. I like the
role of Lady Bountiful. I'm not the least bit interested in spreading around any horse manure.

Recently, however, I've begun to branch
out a bit (tried, but couldn't resist the pun). In
a gardening first, I'm proud to report that I just
cut down a tree—ALL BY MYSELF. It was an
old, ugly holly tree that hadn't produced a berry

since Truman was president. Trust me; it was time for it to go to the big garden in the sky. Something needed to be done about it for years, but we'd never gotten around to it. One morning, as I passed that holly tree on the way to do something else, I was inspired to do something about it myself. I thought: Am I not a healthy, hardy, capable, twenty-first-century kind of woman? Of course, I am! How hard could it possibly be?

I know you are thinking it was really a holly *bush*, but you didn't see it. This was most definitely a big holly *tree*. It could have been decorated with lights and displayed in front of city hall. I'd given up trying to get cuttings from it to use in Christmas decorations because it was like wrestling a bear to cut through each thick limb. That holly tree had lived in my backyard many more years than I had lived in the house. It was rooted. There was nothing tentative about its new growth. Clearly, the holly tree viewed itself as a permanent fixture in the backyard. It wasn't one bit delicate, and it wasn't scared of me and my pruning shears. I was secretly afraid I might have to blast it out of the flowerbed with dynamite.

The whole process took a while. Those holly trees are tougher than they look. I spent the better part of an afternoon tugging on the branches of the holly tree, trying to pull it up by the roots. What a joke. That holly tree wrapped its roots around underground pipes and held on for dear life. I knew it thought if it could just wear me down, I'd give up and go back inside for some consoling sweet tea and cheese straws, but I wasn't in the mood to quit that day. I felt some kind of pioneer spirit channeling through me, and I refused to be bested by a bunch of cellulose.

When I finally triumphed over the foliage, dragged it to the curb, and collapsed on my porch swing, my husband took one look at the stump and said, "I've never seen a stump like that in my life. That looks awful! Did you gnaw it down like a beaver or what?"

I was immediately defensive. "I'd like to see you cut down a tree with pruning shears!" I told him. "I had to finish that sucker off with my fingernail scissors."

The Big White Tent

IF YOU LIVE IN THE SOUTH, AND YOU SEE WORKMEN setting up a big white tent on the front lawn of someone's home, rest assured that the circus is not coming to your neighborhood. That tent means somebody in that house is getting married, and somebody's daddy, mama, or grandmama has been called upon to sign a whole pack of fat checks.

I've been to at least a dozen outside wedding receptions, and I'm still baffled. What is it about the idea of an outside venue for a party that is so appealing to all of us? In order to keep your guests comfortable, you have to spray enough bug killer to contaminate the ground water supply for a generation, and that's just for starters. This mosquito problem ought to be a deal killer all by itself, but it never is.

I admit it. I'm as guilty of falling for the outdoor-party love affair as the next woman, even though I was born and reared in the South. I should know better. I do know better. I know how hot it gets down here on a regular basis. I whine about it all the time. I fully understand that the great outdoors is not air-conditioned. That is why I have a perfectly comfortable home with central air conditioning, several bathrooms, a free-standing icemaker, and every kitchen convenience. The inside of my house is an ideal place for entertaining. Why in the world would I (or anyone I know) plan an outside party where all modern conveniences are in such short supply?

Think about it. This is one of those things lots of people do that doesn't make a bit of sense. There's no good time of the year for an outside wedding reception in the South. Winter is out—too cold. Summer is no good—mosquitoes and perspiration. Fall is tempting. It might be picture-perfect, but it could just as easily be storming, cold, and miserable. It's an even-money bet. There's just no way to predict the weather far enough in advance to make a difference when you're buying seafood by the pound. A spring reception could be glorious, weather-wise, or it could feature hurricane force winds. I tell you there is nothing like tropical force winds to put bridesmaids with complicated hairdos in a bad mood.

It is amazing that even though we know these weather variables, we continue, generation after generation, to plan outdoor receptions. When you think about all the zillion things that can (and do) go wrong at weddings that make everyone miserable, it really makes you wonder about us as a culture. Why do we voluntarily add the outdoor-venue pressure to an already bubbling cauldron full of crazy cousins, step-relations, and assorted ex-relationships? Nevertheless, as soon as an engagement ring has been properly admired, you'll find mothers and daughters making a beeline out the screen door to study the best placement for the tent.

Every time we do that, we attempt to reinvent the wheel. First of all, in case you haven't thought about this important point, remember: there's no kitchen in the great outdoors. This means the caterers have to bring a self-sufficient portable kitchen with them and traipse back and forth between the real kitchen in your house (which has running water and electricity, very helpful kitchen accessories) and the pretend kitchen set up in the tent for the wedding reception. The logistics of keeping fresh shrimp hot or cold, depending on the menu selections, are enough to earn that caterer the first big piece of wedding cake with all the spun-sugar roses he or she can eat.

June brides look a lot less attractive with sweat beads rolling down their backs. Those who splurge on ceiling fans inside the tents deserve a little extra monogramming on their towel presents, in my opinion. In an amazing display of cultural solidarity, Southern women wear full makeup to outside receptions in weather they would not normally go out in except to drape themselves across pool loungers. Sweaty women blotting their foreheads with cocktail napkins are not pretty sights.

In addition to carrying on genteel conversations with mascara running down their cheeks like Tammy Faye Baker on a crying jag, female guests in frivolous party shoes look like they're playing an enormous game of Twister as they pick their way gingerly across the lawn in an effort to avoid another toxic side effect of wedding turmoil: dog poop. If the family dog gets as excited as everyone else during the week leading up to the wedding, you can expect a little tummy upset. Believe me when I tell you that nothing looks worse on dyed *peau de soie* wedding shoes than dog poop.

Of course, there's no parking. It's a private home, not a Wal-mart. There's a driveway with room for four or five cars, at most. Street parking will accommodate another ten cars. That usually takes care of the bride's immediate family—only 256 cars to go. Old people get panicky about parking. Neighbors' flowerbeds are annihilated in a matter of minutes. Tempers flair. Distant cousins forget their manners. Blood feuds are born.

Here's a little news flash: There are no bathrooms outside. Guests have two choices. Option one is the portable potty. Are you really going to ask Great-aunt Mildred, who is ninety-three if she's a day, to use a portable potty when she's had all the lime-green punch she can hold? Imagine squeezing Aunt Mildred, her sizable pocketbook, her wedding hat with the fake flowers on the brim that has been to every family wedding since John Kennedy was president, her walker, and her orthopedic shoes into one of those portable potties and then somehow managing to close the door.

Where in the world will she freshen up her red lipstick, powder her nose, or wash her hands? Is she supposed to leave her hefty handbag outside, propped against the side of the portable potty?

Should she hang it from the branch of a nearby tree? Is she expected to climb into the portable potty right out there behind the tent in sight and hearing of all the party guests? What if the portable potty is sitting on a slant? Think about it. Have you ever been in one that was situated perfectly? Do they even flush? I'm getting worked up just writing about this subject.

Option two is to allow party guests to use the guest bathroom in the bride's home. I ask you: Do you have plumbing in your home that is ready to accommodate four hundred flushing guests and an open bar? This bathroom deal is a disaster waiting to happen. Mark my words.

The only thing good about having a wedding reception outside is the bar situation. You can't beat an outside bar. This is something we do well in the South. Without walls, curtains, and other constraining pieces of heavy antique furniture, we can set up a number of long tables, throw yards of white tablecloths over them, haul in liquor by the U-haul load, and dump a hundred pounds of ice in coolers underneath those tables with ten minutes notice. Add sliced lemons and limes, silver jiggers and pitchers, fancy swizzle sticks, white napkins, and a bartender, and you're in business. If you scatter those bars correctly (there's an art to it; you have to know your party flow), you can ensure that no one has to wait in line for his or her libation of choice. Just between you and me, the easy bar setup is the main reason these outdoor festivities keep happening, in my opinion. That and the fact that guests who are required to stay outside like farm animals rarely flick cigarette ash on the rug or spill red wine on the sofa.

The bottom line is that a tent is still a tent no matter how much it rents for by the hour. Normally, you wouldn't catch a Southern woman voluntarily spending time under a tent unless there are some fine antiques being auctioned under there at rock-bottom prices. For some reason, if you spread out enough exquisite greenery and fresh flower arrangements, keep the booze flowing, and promise a girl she can eat two kinds of cake and dance until dawn under the stars wearing a big white dress, she's a sucker for anything—even an outdoor party with all her relatives.

Mosquitoes

Dᴵᴰ ʏᴏᴜ ᴋɴᴏᴡ ᴛʜᴇʀᴇ ᴀʀᴇ ꜱᴘᴏᴛꜱ ᴏɴ ᴛʜᴇ ɢʟᴏʙᴇ ᴛʜᴀᴛ do not have mosquitoes as native inhabitants?

This has just come to my attention. Frankly, I'm worked up about it. The thought just never occurred to me. As a native Alabamian, I assumed mosquitoes were an inevitable trial of life like taxes, balding, and the common cold.

To think that all I have to do is open an atlas and pick a new place to live and I could be mosquito-free is just about more than my brain can handle.

As a small child sitting in a church pew, I remember hearing a preacher claim that every living thing has a divine and glorious purpose in life. Even though I was not tall enough to see over the pew in front of me, my first thought was: *hogwash.*

I defy you to find a divine role for mosquitoes. I read some vague justification for their existence in *National Geographic*, but, frankly, it wasn't that earth-shattering. I think we'd all rock along just fine without the little bloodsuckers.

Now that I think about it, what's so glorious about cockroaches? The idea that roaches and Styrofoam are the only things that might survive a nuclear attack is interesting, maybe, but not divine.

This Old Yard

WE ARE LUCKY TO LIVE IN A COMFORTABLE, reasonably attractive home in a safe suburb. I say lucky because I am well aware that this is not a reality for everyone. We were somehow wise enough when we were scraping together coins from the sofa cushions to come up with the down payment on our first house to listen to agents urging us to buy with regard to location, location, location. We paid attention and bought a charming, cottage starter home with lots of curb appeal nestled on a hot street. We later sold that two-bedroom, one-bath house for a profit that allowed us to buy our second home, the one we still live in today. I loved it the day we bought it, and I still love it today.

You can stand on the front porch of the house we live in now and see a bit of our first house a block away. We're committed to the neighborhood. We were awfully young when we made that first home purchase. It was a lucky buy. We could just as easily have bought a charming fixer-upper crack house in the flood plain out by the airport. We were babes in the woods. Still, I'm glad we chose well—for my children, who are counting on us to pay their college tuition.

In many ways, I think being happily married, like stumbling into a good house purchase the first time around, is mostly a product of sheer, dumb luck, too. I know that doesn't sound romantic, and I'm not saying it doesn't take a lot of work to keep a relationship humming along (or even limping or lurching along, upon occasion).

In our country, most of us marry young. We rarely ask the important questions about family, money, children, etc. We just decide we're in love with someone and, before you know it, we're making life-long promises, fearsome pledges until death does us part, and signing up for a tour of duty that includes sickness and health—and a lot of other things we can't even imagine when we're twenty-two, healthy, attractive, skinny, driving a car our parents paid for, and seeing the dermatologist once a month on somebody else's health-insurance plan.

When I read that marriages in America based on the "in love" plan have no more chance, statistically, at a happy ending than arranged marriages in other countries where your first sight of the person you are going to spend the next fifty years sleeping next to is a furtive glimpse thirty minutes before the ceremony, well, it didn't surprise me a bit. The whole deal is still pretty haphazard.

It amazes me that you can dissolve a marriage in this country so easily, too. I think many immature individuals simply get in a fight and turn that into a quick, inexpensive, huffy divorce. And if you think divorced women in our country have it rough, you need to do a little reading about what happens to divorced women in some far-flung parts of the globe. From everything I've read, however, it seems like the divorced men seem to make out just fine, regardless of their culture, religion, or country. Once again, let me say: this does not surprise me at all.

Our house reminds me of an old, comfortable marriage. It's not picture perfect, but there's something appealing about it. It is a brick, Tudor-style house, about eighty-years-old, with wonderful old, wavy glass in the windows (well, the glass a baseball hasn't passed through), heavy stone accents, and a steep roof with a number of peaks and valleys. That's interesting for those of us on the ground admiring the antique-slate color of the roof tiles. I don't think the charm factor was nearly as appealing to the roofers who attached ropes to their waists and repelled down the sides of my roof when we had to have some repair work done. They looked pretty grim. It frightened me just to watch them. I went inside and made a pitcher of tea and sliced up a pound cake for their break. They earned it. The whole charm package is lost on roofers, I suspect, and I can't say I blame them.

You might logically expect that to go along with our quaint old house we'd have a pretty impressive lawn with interesting gates, accent pieces, well-established foliage, and well-worn garden benches tucked away. In a way, you'd be right. We do have well-established foliage. That is to say, we have old bushes and trees. They are certainly well established because they haven't been pruned or trimmed in years. I know that during the fall leaf season, it looks like nobody lives here. You have to clear a path through the leaves to get to the front door, and if you're smart, you'll blaze your trail on tree trunks along the way like a boy scout so you can find your way back out to your car. We just don't have the time or the talent or the money to do anything about our yard. Around here, with three children, my husband and I found that something had to give. We decided to give up on the yard. We mow it just enough to not get calls from the neighbors, and that's about it.

Just because we have an old, well-established yard doesn't mean it looks good. This might be a good place to remind you that not everything old is a valuable antique. For example, I guess some of that trash in Elvis's house in Memphis will approach antique status soon. That doesn't make it any more attractive. They made junk in every era, you know. Bad taste isn't any more attractive with age. Sometimes, old is just old.

Someday, my husband and I will attend to the yard. I promise. Until then, we're attending to the kids and each other. We'd like to publicly apologize to all those who view our yard as a community eyesore. We're open to suggestions, and we're doing the best we can. Honest.

Six Reasons Not to Plan an Outdoor Wedding

I see the temptation. I really do. Twenty years ago, I had an outdoor wedding myself. If everything goes off without a hitch, they're very picturesque. They're also chock-full of disasters just waiting to happen. When you feel the urge to plan an outdoor wedding for yourself or your child, remind yourself of all the terrible things that could happen. Just because you assume those things will never happen to you doesn't mean they won't, you know. Think of your family. Think of your friends. Have mercy. An outdoor wedding is a pain in the behind for everybody involved. When you find yourself tempted by Japanese lanterns and summer breezes, remind yourself of the following pitfalls, and resist the urge!

1) Have you been living under a rock? Didn't you get the newsflash about global warming? We're going to get more and more tornadoes, hurricanes, floods, mudslides, tsunamis—the whole nine yards. All the experts agree. Do you really want the mother of the bride to have to worry about an evacuation plan for her reception guests?

2) Do you want to end up on television in one of those *America's Funniest Home Videos* episodes? I can tell you that if I was the groom tumbling down the hillside or the bride getting soaked by a big wave at a beach wedding, I would not be amused. If I was the bridesmaid with bird poop running off the brim of my mint-green wedding hat, I can tell you I wouldn't find it nearly as funny as watching the wedding misfortune of strangers on television. I bet you wouldn't either.

3) Do I have to talk about the lack of bathroom and kitchen facilities again? If you are thinking about an outdoor wedding, you need to get over it. Right now.

4) June wedding receptions are supposed to be held indoors in the South. That is why God made air conditioning. Period.

5) Have you noticed the shoe styles women wear to weddings in the South? Do they look like hiking boots to you? There's a *reason* for that. They're delicate, thinly heeled, and dyed to match all manner of dresses, wraps, and handbags. They're not designed for

a strenuous workout. Wedding shoes should come with labels that say "Valet Parking Only" because a waxed, parquet dance floor is the harshest terrain they're equipped to handle.

6) Have you thought about the wildlife that may show up, uninvited, to graze at your buffet table? Mosquitoes, bees, yellow jackets, hornets, fire ants, roaches, moths, ladybugs, odious black flies, beetles, crickets, grasshoppers, and other flying things I don't know the names of are reason enough to scuttle outside wedding plans.

Not to mention SNAKES. Of course, there are snakes out there. "Out there" is where snakes *live*. Where do you think they're going to be on the night of your wedding? Do you think they're going to reserve hotel rooms out of town so they won't disturb your festivities? You better hope the bride doesn't step right on top of a cottonmouth on her dash to the goin' away car. A bride with a big toe swollen to the size of a cantaloupe would not be a pretty sight on her honeymoon trip to Hawaii.

You also have to worry about opossums, raccoons, dogs, cats, squirrels, and birds. They call the great outdoors where you're planning your party home, too. I hate to even think about the possibilities posed by the presence of cows, horses, and, mercy me, *bulls*. If some creature can get loose, it will. You know it's bound to happen. If there is an endangered wild boar left out there in the woods, you can count on him cutting into the buffet line, and he's not going to be too pleased when he sees his second cousin dead as a doornail on a platter with an apple stuck in its mouth.

Now that I think about it, what if the outdoor wedding venue is near a hunting preserve? Are you comfortable with a deer or two wandering over to check out the appetizer table? Now, I love Bambi to death, but I believe that back-to-nature experience is one your wedding guests would just as soon skip.

Somewhere out there is a hostess who's had to worry about buffalo knocking over her flower arrangements. I'm sure of it. Around the globe, I'm sure there are wedding planners forced to shoo away herds of camels, rhinos, and a stray emu or two. It's a wild kingdom out there.

That's why cavemen came up with the concept of *shelter*. It's a sobering realization when you think about the fact that there's not much more than four plaster walls separating us from the rest of God's creatures. I say we keep it that way. It's better for everybody involved.

Curious Characters

Setting the Table

ONE THING I LOVE ABOUT SOUTHERNERS IS OUR ability to appreciate those among us who are a little bit different than the rest of us. I think our well-developed sense of humor allows us to enjoy the quirks, eccentricities, and slightly odd behavior of relatives, friends, and neighbors and adds a level of richness and depth to all of our lives. Maybe it comes from an early realization that we're stuck with our weird cousins, aunts, uncles, and in-laws for life, so we're more receptive to people who have their own ways of doing things—ways that might get them locked up or institutionalized in another part of the country.

It's a philosophical passivity that has something to do with the heat, I think. You can't worry about everything. So your great-grandmother likes to exercise naked on the porch—who is she really hurting? How many voyeurs enjoy an eyeful of an old, wrinkled, saggy lady? Not that many, I suspect. Believe it or not, I actually know a true story about an old woman who exercised naked on her porch about twice a week in the town where I grew up. If I'd been carrying a bag of groceries past her house on those mornings, I would have turned my head the other way and ignored it. To me, that seems like the polite way to handle the situation.

I don't spend any time wondering *why* she exercised naked on the porch. Her great-granddaughter and I have talked that topic to death. I'm over the shock factor. I've got things to do. Besides, deep down, we all know why she exercised naked. She was a little bit crazy. Her mama was a little bit crazy, too. I never heard that she exercised naked on the porch, but she did other crazy things, like collect church bulletins. She had shoeboxes full of them.

Upon reflection, I don't think naked porch exercising is that big of a deal. There are a lot worse things someone could get up to than exercising naked on the porch or collecting church bulletins. It probably got hot exercising on that porch. You can't believe how hot it gets in Alabama if you're not from here.

I'll be the first to admit that crazy people are sometimes scary. Most of the time, however, they're not hurting anyone. Their behavior is best described as a little odd. Occasionally, dementia or genetic craziness can be sweet. If you let yourself go with the flow a bit around a crazy person, it can be a liberating experience. I learned that on the day I'm just about to describe. I know it takes a while to come around to appreciating the funny side of dementia, but I say it's worth a try. Usually, there's not a thing you can do about dementia anyway.

I have an elderly neighbor across the street who lives far away from her children and other extended family members. She tells me all the time that the hardest thing about being in her nineties is that she has outlived almost all of her friends. Many of her friends who are still alive can't drive and don't get out of the house much, or they don't remember who she is or who they are anymore. She says this is more depressing than the friends who are dead. I see her point.

She worries there will be no one to come to her funeral when she dies. She says she could have really had an impressive send-off if she had died a decade or so ago. She hates that none of her friends will be able to attend, and she fears that a member of the clergy who never knew her will eulogize her in all the wrong ways. I have promised her I will go to her funeral, and I will bring a friend with me. I've offered to deliver her eulogy to make sure it is a testament to the great fun she says she had in her life. I've told her I'll try to get the priest to stick to the *Book of Common Prayer*. We're both Episcopalian, and we believe it's hard to mess up a funeral if you stick to the playbook. Unfortunately, we've both been to funerals where the preacher was more concerned with his own ego than with celebrating the deceased's life. Just a few years ago, we went to the funeral of another neighbor, and it was a travesty. It was obvious to both of us within the first five minutes that the preacher had never met our neighbor. She'd have been appalled at his hijacking of her service as an excuse to evangelize her mourners. It was a lot like being invited to a dinner party only to arrive and discover the hostess is actually selling Tupperware.

My current neighbor was scandalized. She thought his eulogy was a cheap shot and gave short shrift to our deceased neighbor. I agreed with her. We talked about it all the way home in the car. We both agree that if you can't say anything nice about someone at a wedding or funeral, then why in the world would you agree to speak at all? With a little effort, I feel sure we can all find something nice to say about everyone. If not, a wedding or funeral would be a good time to make something up. Clearly, this would be an opportunity to exercise discretion, good manners, and creativity. Getting even with someone in a casket is as low as you can possibly go.

Most days, my neighbor is still pretty sharp, mentally. I try to check on her at least once a day. She always answers the same way when I knock on her door or call out to her from the porch: "I'm here; I'm not dead yet!" You have to love a woman with a sense of humor like that. I certainly do.

She does have a few quirks. These days, she has a lot of time on her hands. She used to love to entertain, and her favorite hostess activity was throwing a dinner party. I've heard her descriptions of some of her favorite parties, and I've even tried to re-create a few of her recipes. It is obvious she and her friends had a ton of fun. You can just tell.

My favorite story she tells is about a dinner party she had during an epic storm when all the power went out. She couldn't cook a thing, so she cut up the meat, put it on skewers with the vegetables she was going to serve, and they roasted it on coat hangers over the fireplace in the living room. She kept the drinks flowing, and she swears she and all her girlfriends looked even more ravishing by candlelight. I love to watch her face when she tells that story. She gets this twinkle in her eyes, and I can look into them and see a glimpse of what she must have been like in her prime. She was a ringleader, no question about it—always up for everything, no matter what time it was, and regardless of what she had to get up and do the next morning.

She is not up to hostessing parties anymore, but she says that's okay because there is no one she wants to invite anyway. Nevertheless, strictly for her own entertainment, every day or two she sets the table for a dinner party. Sometimes, she sets it two or three different times in one day. She's not delusional. She doesn't think anyone is actually going to show up to eat. She just likes to pretend. While she is busy setting the table, I think she remembers the laughter and good times of previous decades.

The first time I walked into her dining room and discovered the lay of the land, I didn't know what to think. The table looked divine. It was set for eight with a gorgeous set of Sevres china that hasn't been sold in stores in a couple of generations. She was working on a centerpiece in a huge, footed, Waterford crystal bowl with greenery and hydrangeas from her yard. She was adding long stems of eucalyptus from a bush that grows in her front flowerbed, a bush that I covet and have asked her to expressly will to me when she dies. She agreed, of course, chiefly because she said she knew she wouldn't even be laid out in the funeral home before I'd be over in her flowerbed digging the whole bush up and moving it over to my own yard anyway. This I hotly denied. I'd have waited until the house was about to be sold. Then, I'd have stolen it.

My neighbor is a gifted flower arranger, and she has helped me out of some flower-arranging emergencies in the past, so I immediately went to stand right by her to watch every step of her current project. She always keeps a running commentary going while she arranges. If you pay attention, you can learn a lot.

"There," she said, giving the last stem a tweak, "what do you think?"

"I think it's perfect, and you know it," I replied. "I don't know how you do it!"

"I pay attention," she always says. "Flowers tell you how to arrange them if you just pay attention. Look at how they're growing, leaning. You can see it."

"My flowers don't say anything to me," I told my neighbor. "Maybe I heard a faint cry for help one time. . . ."

Leaning against her shoulder, I said, a little nervously, "You know nobody is actually coming to dinner, right?"

"Of course I know! I'm not senile yet!" she answered.

"Then I think this table is absolutely divine," I told her.

"I agree," she says, "nothing more I can do here, but I have a little surprise for you. Next, I'm going to do a pretend Christmas dinner! You can help!"

Well, of course, I ran home as fast as I could to see if I still had any holly berries hanging on for dear life at the end of March. I rummaged through my sideboard looking for Christmas candles and finally decided that if we were going that far, I should get down the Christmas nativity pieces. There's no telling what my neighbor could do with spring greenery and a baby Jesus. How many times do you get the opportunity to set a Christmas table in March? I know a good thing when I see it.

As I dashed out of the front door with a wreath on each arm, baby Jesus in my pocket, and a couple of red candles in each hand, my husband asked, over the top of his newspaper, "What are y'all doing over there?"

"We're setting the table for Christmas dinner!" I answered enthusiastically. By this point, I was totally on board with my neighbor's game. I ask you: how many times do you get to play house as an adult? We were having a ball.

"*Okay* . . . " he said, totally missing out on the spirit of the adventure.

Belatedly, he realized that the Southern women around him were behaving oddly—even for us. "Hey!" he yelled through the screen door to my hurrying back. "Do y'all even know it's March over there?" he asked, thinking he was oh-so-witty.

"Yep. We know," I assured him over my shoulder, "what difference does it make?"

"Just trying to help," I heard him mutter huffily as I opened my neighbor's door with one finger and tried to squeeze in sideways so I wouldn't drop my Christmas paraphernalia.

"I haven't even told you the best part yet," my neighbor said with a big grin on her face and her hands clasped gleefully together in front of her.

"Let's hear it!" I demanded.

"No dishes!" she announced triumphantly.

This game just got better and better. We had spent the better part of an hour having a great time discussing our table options before moving on to the dining-room sideboard when we heard a knock at the front door.

"I'll see who it is," I told my neighbor.

"What is it?" I asked my husband. I was in a hurry to get back to my play date.

"Y'all are having too much fun over here. I just came over to see if you need me to put up the Christmas lights or something."

I tell you there is just something about that man that I like.

A Little Different

WE HAVE ALL SORTS OF EUPHEMISMS FOR CRAZY people down here. I guess you know you're not supposed to call crazy people "crazy" anymore. It's not polite. Mental illness is, of course, a serious disease, one that causes infinite heartache for everyone involved. Long before the advent of sensitivity seminars and politically correct speech, we already had different ways of referring to crazy people in the South without calling them crazy or hurting their feelings. That "crazy" word gets bandied about in common name calling a good bit. I admit that I wouldn't like to be called crazy one bit, even if I was certifiable, so I understand the objection.

The problem is there are still a lot of crazy people out there. In addition, there are even more individuals among us who are not technically mentally ill, but who are, however, still a sandwich short of a picnic, or not quite all there, people whose elevator doesn't go all the way to the top. You know what I mean.

My favorite euphemism for crazy people is a Southern collo-
quialism. Down here, we often say, "She's just a little different." It
sounds nicer than, "She's crazy as a loon." There is a whole world
of people who fit in this category, and it applies to a large number of ordinary people out in public going about their regular lives.
They don't have a medical diagnosis. They just have a few quirks
we all need to work around. After all, who among us doesn't have a
few quirks? For example, I think it is perfectly normal that I refuse
to try and parallel park my Suburban, but if I lived somewhere else
in the country, that little quirk might be evidence used to lock me
up for some kind of study. I'm not about to cast any stones. My
house is made of delicate crystal. I have lots of little eccentricities.
I like to think it's all part of the whole charm package.

Perhaps because of my own personality quirks, I seem to at-
tract people who are a little bit different. If there is a person who
marches to the beat of a different drummer (or even an invisible
drummer) within a hundred miles of me, he or she will sit down by
me and strike up a conversation or embark upon a lengthy mono-
logue that makes me want to gather up my children and hide them
under the hem of my dress.

Since this is the South, and we have a significant number of
nut cases in our own families—not to mention the random eccen-
trics we come in contact with at church, school, work, etc.—my
crazy-magnet personality trait is a constant problem. If I am in a
crowded movie theater, and one paranoid person arrives to rave at
the movie actors who he is certain are trying to take over the world,
he will sit by me and search my movie popcorn for hidden microphones. No doubt about it. The odds could have been two hundred
to one, and it wouldn't matter. I could be window-shopping with
thousands of other people on a crowded city street, but the bizarre,
world's-about-to-end people will crowd around me to demand some
answers.

One time when I got my hair cut, I somehow became involved
in my crazy hair stylist's woes regarding her lazy, truck-driving husband who won't leave her overnight to work because he is afraid she
will cheat on him. She says she won't do this because she cheated
on her first husband, and now she is "reaping what she sowed,"

and, anyway, since then, she has FOUND THE LORD. If you could hear her say that, you would know it should be typed in capital letters. Now, I don't doubt her religious experience for a minute. What I don't understand is why she has to share it with *me*.

I have tried the usual defenses. I was ostentatiously reading a book at the beauty parlor, and I never ask crazy people questions. I say "aha" and "umhm" and "I see" over and over. Nevertheless, something about me makes them feel the need to share their special problems with me in a loud voice and in a public place. Perhaps they recognize that deep inside I am one of their own. I'm a little bit worried about that.

The crazy-person etiquette dilemma is that I am a Southern woman, and I don't want to be rude, even in potentially dangerous situations. This means, of course, that a crazy person has a captive audience with me. I feel sorry for them. Who wouldn't? It can't be much fun to live a life where strangers avoid you as much as possible. I know I'm an easy mark. I probably would have invited Ted Bundy in for coffee.

As a consequence, I end up embroiled in domestic disputes, counseling sessions, employment solicitations, and assorted other dead-end situations that are none of my business. My husband now makes a face when he hears the words, "What could we do about ——?" I don't want to counsel crazy people. I'm not educated for it. I'm not good at it. I can't understand why I keep stumbling over their problems like landmines.

I've found that during the holiday seasons, it really isn't too much trouble to invite a social misfit to a family gathering. I always say you can seat the crazy people near the hard-of-hearing crowd. Depending on your family make-up, you can have your own crazy table and mix up the chemically dependent with the chemically un-balanced. I could probably come up with some snazzy place cards for that table. At the very least, a few loons added to a holiday meal will give everyone something new to talk about. As a good Southern hostess, I like to keep the conversation flowing, and there is nothing quite like a nut case to jumpstart the repartee.

Leila's Envelopes

I AM CONSTANTLY AMAZED WHENEVER I DISCOVER something new about a person I have known for years. It's shocking how often ordinary people like us are involved in extraordinary events. Some of these activities are so unusual and interesting I find it hard to believe no one ever told me about them before. Everybody who knows me knows I want to hear just about everything in the world.

Just last summer, I found myself sitting next to another mom in a ballpark when I discovered through our casual conversation that she had won an Olympic gold medal for rowing. Well. I wanted to make an announcement on the public address system. How exciting! I've discovered that if you ask the people around you a few questions, you'll be amazed by what you find out. There are a lot of extraordinary people living right smack dab in the middle of us ordinary citizens.

We all know stories about heroes who've

never been more than twenty miles from home until they go off to war and distinguish themselves half a world away in ways that those of us who knew them could never have imagined. Natural disasters, wars, births, deaths, fires, car accidents—all are catalysts for extraordinary courage, selflessness, and heroism. News reports are full of those stories.

Unfortunately, the converse is also true. While horrific circumstances bring out the very best we humans have to offer, they also bring out the very worst of our human traits: greed and selfishness. Think about hurricane price-gouging vultures or citizens who look the other way in times of ethnic or religious cleansing. I believe the good news is that there are more good people than bad. I'm sticking with this story, and there's nothing you can say to change my mind. I have to believe that in order to get up in the morning and start the day with a smile.

In the past, I think we have all heard more about extraordinary men than women. Maybe that's because of the nature of their heroism or sacrifice, but I think it goes deeper than that. I think much of the history of women, Southern women in particular, hasn't been written down. It is a rare occasion when we stumble upon a woman's surprising life story. We are forced to look at that woman in a completely different way than we have ever seen her before. I love when that happens.

Women have complex roles in our society. They rarely have one career, one clearly delineated identity. Over the years, Southern women have had to be adaptable. They've sometimes had to plant their own food, grow it, harvest it, can it, serve it up to their husbands and children, and give their husbands all the credit. Southern women are sometimes overlooked and taken for granted. It often takes a generation or two for their contributions to be fully appreciated. I just found out some surprising details about the life of an ordinary Alabama woman. I'm a little piqued that I had never in my life heard the story before. It blew my socks off. She's a character.

Her name is Leila. She's old now and suffering from dementia. She knows her children when she sees them, but, more and more, her daily preoccupation goes back more than eighty years to her childhood in Selma, Alabama. She asks about her mother a lot.

She wants to go home, and home, in her mind, is where she grew up. Leila's story is ordinary in so many ways. The woes of aging are universal and inevitable—if we're lucky enough to get that far. I was reminded this week of something we often forget. I was reminded of the life that Leila lived before she got old. It's worth remembering. She's worth remembering. All those women who came before us are worth remembering.

I love that just when you think you know everything there is to know about someone, you find out something that amazes you. For example, Leila played in a semi-professional basketball league back in the 1930s. She was known to give her son and his friends basketball tips when they were growing up, and she could still dribble to the basket and make a lay-up on her eightieth birthday. The league traveled all over Alabama and Mississippi. She remembers, sometimes, hilarious tales about the small towns they visited. She remembers the twin girls, Mona and Merle, who both played guard. The teams played half-court back then with three on a side. Leila, as you might expect, was the ringleader at center. Then World War II came along; everyone got married, and life moved on.

Leila was adaptable. Always an athlete, she traveled all the way to North Carolina to get certified by the American Red Cross as a swimming instructor. In her small town, she taught hundreds of boys and girls to swim. There was a picture of her in the newspaper diving off the new diving board. She helped start up a women's softball team. They played on the little-league field. When the exercise-class craze became popular, she checked out books from the library and read magazines to learn how to run those classes herself. To this day, the First Baptist Church still shows the videotape of her leading the exercise class. No one else wants to take over her job. She must have been some kind of teacher! I'm told by reliable sources that she believed in a *strenuous* workout.

A while back, Leila called her son to tell him she had something she wanted to show him. She took him over to a cedar chest, which had sat in one spot for as long as he could remember, and said, "Look in there." When he opened the lid, he could see stacks of just what he'd expected to see: clothes. Deep inside, he saw something else, a white plastic bag like the ones you get at the grocery store, the drugstore, or Wal-mart to take your purchases home. "Look inside," she told him.

Inside the plastic bag were sixty or seventy identical, small, brown envelopes, the kind you used to receive when you bought buttons, the kind of envelopes children use to enclose their church tithe before dropping it into the offering plate on Sunday morning. The envelopes were unsealed. On the outside of each envelope, in his mother's lovely script, penmanship he could identify just as easily in a hundred years, each envelope was labeled. The first one he picked up said, "Leftover vacation money, Panama City, 1953." When he opened the flap, a few dollars and some change spilled out into his hand.

"What do you want me to do with this, Mama?" he asked, "Do you want me to put it in the bank for you?"

"Yes, whatever you think is best. I don't want anything to happen to it," she told him.

It was a small request. He was happy to do it for her. He didn't think too much about it.

When he got home that night, he poured the contents of the bag onto his dining room table. There were many more envelopes than he'd originally thought. There were too many to count. For hours, he revisited his childhood in a catalog of spidery writing on the outside of the envelopes. He read dates, places, and events that he knew about and some he never knew about or didn't pay attention to as a child. For over an hour, he poured the contents of the envelopes into his palm and recorded the results on a pad of paper. Some envelopes held just a few dollars, others as much as twenty-two or three. The high-end envelope held forty dollars. While he was recording, he was reliving his childhood. What kind of trip had his mother made to Colorado in 1963? He couldn't remember. A dollar here and there—pretty soon, he began to add it all up.

When he was finished, he sat back in his chair, dumbfounded. Over the course of an entire lifetime, his mother had saved thirteen thousand dollars, a nickel, dime, and quarter at a time. Nobody knew about Leila's envelopes. Her husband didn't know; her children didn't either.

It seemed impossible. For years, she'd worked the notions

counter at Planter's Mercantile Company. She was known around town as a gifted seamstress, and local women regularly asked her for sewing advice. I can remember going to the back of the store to the counter where she worked when I was a child. I can see the smooth, uneven wood of the counter, which was at my eye-level, and I can see in my mind her fingers measuring off fabric from the bolt against the yardstick fixed to the counter.

Her employer allowed her to sell the things she sewed at home in the notions section in the back of the store. The envelopes showed evidence of years of piecework. One envelope said "ribbons," another "buttons"; one said, "zippers."

Every penny she made, she saved. She spent nothing. She made all her own clothes. One of her son's earliest memories is watching his mother cut out patterns on their dining table. He can still picture the thin, brown, tissue pattern pieces and the shiny straight pins she used to secure each piece to the fabric.

Leila was a depression-era product. Regardless of the hardships of her day, she was convinced she would need the money more sometime in the future. She saved and saved and saved. When she became old enough to receive social security benefits, she was suspicious. Because she was still working, she was convinced the government would one day show up on her doorstep and demand the money back, so she never spent it. Not a penny. It sat in her checking account month after month, year after year.

In a way she was right. Now that money is coming in handy. With little envelopes of a few dollars each, she pays for her nursing care now. Over the years, leftover vacation money and money earned putting zippers in other people's dresses, covering a few buttons, and making a couple of bows added up to a unique savings plan. Her son finally convinced her to buy CDs with the social security money. She made a little interest. So far, it's been enough to take care of her. With the hard work of her own two hands, by continuing to be active and flexible, Leila took care of her own future. I'm humbled by the thought of Leila's envelopes—by the way she lived her life.

I like her style.

Doug's Shoes

HAVE YOU EVER NOTICED HOW THE SMALLEST DETAIL about someone's appearance can be the perfect metaphor for the whole person? One Sunday, I was transfixed by one such detail—my Episcopal priest's shoes.

Shoes are usually a good reflection of their owner's life. What else do you really need to know about Imelda Marcos, for example? The shoe greed just about sums her up; wouldn't you agree?

The first thing I noticed about my priest's shoes is they are very large. I would guess a size twelve, at least. And they are very worn. In all the years I have known him, I do not think I have ever noticed him wearing a new pair of shoes. (Frankly, I tend to notice a priest's shoes since the rest of the uniform is pretty standard issue, except for the colorful, seasonal stole additions.)

For a few minutes, I puzzled over their well-worn shape. The toes are bowed up like he frequently rocks back and forth from heel to toe.

Eventually, I realized they are *prayer* worn. Their odd shape is the result of hours and hours spent on his knees, service after service, day after day.

Doug's shoes are plain black. They have a comfortable sole and little shine. They are an inexpensive, nondescript pair of shoes for humble feet. As I sat in the pew, I thought about how many miles that size-twelve pair of shoes walked during the previous week, about how many times he rolled those shoes to their tips to pray on his aging knees, about the prestigious and humble homes all over the parish that he visited while wearing them.

I thought about the people who were comforted by the sight of that worn tread and the hospital corridors those shoes traveled. I reflected upon the grains of dirt from hundreds of cemeteries those shoes must have embedded in their soles. I wondered about the conversations those feet were still and silent long enough to hear.

I bet those well-worn shoes took Doug comfortably to California a few years ago when he performed the marriage ceremony for a famous actress as easily as they took him to the poorest homes in Birmingham, Alabama. At my very first book signing, I looked up from the table where I was signing books, and I saw those big shoes waiting patiently in line. I was so pleased to see him there! It was the nicest surprise I could imagine.

I am ashamed to confess that I have more shoes than I can count. I have shoes I can't wear anymore but haven't given away. I have shoes bought to court fashion trends in years gone by that I wouldn't be caught dead in today. Not one pair of my shoes has the character of Doug's Sunday shoes. Not one pair shows the priorities of my life the way that Doug's do. Doug's shoes are a study in character, in humility, in the blessedness that comes from attending with care and patience to the most ordinary among us.

I have been thinking about the shoes of all the people in my life and how revealing they are. Even my children's first baby shoes, carefully saved in their trunks, shoes marked by scuffs and scrapes as my children learned the laws of gravity, tell a story.

I think about the wide, work-worn, clumsily shod feet of the domestic workers I see every morning at the bus stop on our walk to school. I think of my husband's black dress shoes, the same style he has worn since I met him over twenty years ago. They are a testament to his conservative nature, his steadfastness.

I think about my own shoes. Clearly, the ones I have on today were made for comfort since they make zero fashion statement. I am, however, quite pleased to report they both match today. They have flecks of paint on them from a school art project. They have ballpark mud caked on the bottom of their soles. In addition, you can see a few cupcake sprinkles from last week in the crevices of one shoe. In short, my shoes are dirty, dull, and decidedly unimpressive.

Maybe Doug would let me tramp around in his size twelves for a while. Some of that goodness might just rub off. In fact, I am sure Doug would say it might be good for all of us to do a bit of walking in someone else's shoes. It sure would be hard to find feet big enough to fill Doug's big shoes—literally and metaphorically.

Miss Kendrick

ONCE WHEN I WAS ADDRESSING INVITATIONS FOR A party I was giving along with several other hostesses, I paused when I came across the name Kendrick on the honoree's guest list. I laughed to myself for a moment at the instant image the name conjured in my mind of a teacher from my childhood, a woman many years deceased, one of those teachers who left an impression on me for the rest of my life.

She was called Miss Kendrick, even though she was married to a perfectly respectable small-town doctor, because this is the South, and "Miss" is a gesture of respect, not an indicator of marital status at all, at least as far as spoken English is concerned. She would have been more formally and correctly addressed as "Mrs. James Kendrick" in writing. (All this is needless explanation for you Southerners who wonder why I am treating you like a preschooler, but I have readers from other parts of the country, too, you know. I have to clarify things when I get a little too colloquial.)

I first met Miss Kendrick in kindergarten. She was one of my two teachers. I don't remember much about her then except that good manners ranked high on her curriculum. Later on, she taught me Latin and French because I am from a small town, and back then, schools used all the local talent they could find.

I remember funny little things about Miss Kendrick. Probably they are not all true, but this is how I remember them.

I know that she was considered a properly finished young woman in her day. She was a coed at the University of Alabama at sixteen—imagine! She told us that her hair turned solid white while she was still in her twenties. She was always a teeny-tiny woman who seemed to shrink even more with age.

Miss Kendrick had two pairs of cat-eye glasses that appeared to be expensive but were horribly unfashionable at the time. They would undoubtedly be *tres chic* again today. One pair was tinted for sun protection, and the other pair held clear lenses. Every time she came in the classroom, she carefully removed the sunglasses and put them in a case in her pocketbook, a relic of bygone days that looked like something Queen Elizabeth II would carry around on her arm. She carried it, just so, at the crook of her bent elbow. I can still hear the sound of that handbag snapping closed, the sound of a class ready to commence, a sound that still prompts me to involuntarily begin conjugating French verbs.

She wore neatly tailored suits every day, not a wardrobe with much variety but one of excellent quality. She would have made Miss Chanel proud. Miss Kendrick wore medium-heeled pumps and constantly rose up to her tiptoes and rolled back down again as she patrolled the room with her ruler listening to her students learning by rote. Eventually, all her shoes were turned up like tiny elf shoes, and when she stood with her feet together, her toes were always slightly turned out like a little girl who has carefully formed the first position in ballet class.

When I heard Miss Kendrick had died, the first thing that came to my mind was a vision of those boxes of little shoes with the turned-up toes that someone would now pack up and give away.

She was so small that every high-school male—and most of the females—in the classroom dwarfed her, but she had no real problem maintaining discipline. She was the epitome of a Southern lady. You wouldn't think of offending her sensibilities.

Towards the end of her teaching career, she began to forget things. Her language skills were not as sharp as they once were. She kept her desk drawer open just enough to let her peek inside at the answers as she quizzed us. I am certain she thought she was incredibly clandestine, but obnoxious, sharp little teenagers that we were, of course, we knew.

Miss Kendrick had such terrible arthritis in her hands that she was ashamed of them and always tucked them into her pockets or clasped them together behind her back. She often said her hands were a trial to her.

Miss Kendrick had a favorite word, and every student who was ever in her class knows it well. The word was "decorum." She demanded decorum at all times and in all activities. She would have decorum. Period. The end.

Mostly, she got it.

I have a great affection for the word decorum now because of Miss Kendrick. You can blame her for the frequent appearance of that word in my vocabulary. Ergo, you have to read about it. As you can see, a few years in Miss Kendrick's Latin class were dangerous. The word decorum just seems to be the perfect noun for so many situations that I find myself in—the absence of decorum, the need for decorum, and the value of decorum. It's hard to get in trouble using the word decorum. Just saying it makes me stand up straighter and remember to cross my legs at my ankles.

After I grew up and became a teacher, I thought about Miss Kendrick sometimes, and I can't really explain why. She was not, overtly, at least, a terribly influential teacher in my life. We had no special bond. I doubt she would have remembered me, particularly.

What amazes me to this day about Miss Kendrick is that she epitomizes for me so much that is lost in our institutionalized school setting today. She was gracious, well mannered, well educated, and well read. She taught joyfully and responsibly. Today, I doubt she would be hired. Certainly, she would not have the freedom to teach life lessons I remember much more than the "*amo, amas, amat*" Latin conjugations that fly up from my memory at the sound of her name.

I think often of the years that I taught other people's children before my own were born. I sincerely hope I was a Miss Kendrick for some of my own students.

I seem to recall that Miss Kendrick had a granddaughter. Wouldn't it be strange if the woman on my invitation list turns out to be Miss Kendrick's progeny? Odd how life comes full circle sometimes, isn't it?

How did SWAG Come to Be?

The first book, *SWAG: Southern Women Aging Gracefully*, was an accident. It began with one woman's struggle to find meaning, worth, and happiness in the delightfully ordinary trials of everyday life as a stay-at-home mom in the South. After teaching college-aged kids for years, staying home with my own small children came as something of a shock.

When I began writing a monthly letter, it was just for fun, a lark, entertainment for twenty or so friends and an intellectually stimulating exercise for me. I never intended to begin a small business in my dining room, but I discovered an almost insatiable appetite out there for a writer who could give a voice to a mostly overlooked segment of the population—ordinary Southern women.

Regular subscribers wanted to send subscriptions to girlfriends, mothers, and sisters all over until I was running an accidentally created small business with thousands of readers in thirty-eight states! I still have a laundry basket of letters from people all over who all told me the same thing: "I feel like you are writing about my life!"

I feel that I am more a stenographer than a writer, someone who just happens to be paying attention and writing about events as they unfold. I know hundreds of women who could write the same stories if they had the time and the inclination and the patience and the courage to TELL THE TRUTH.

I love to talk to readers. The most common question they ask is, "Did that really happen?" I have a standard response; I say, "Not everything I write is factual, but it's all absolutely true." I've never met a woman who didn't know exactly what I meant by that. I'll leave it up to librarians to decide whether to put me on the fiction or nonfiction shelf because that is really a cosmic question, in my mind, and a whole lot bigger than the Dewey Decimal system.

READING GROUP GUIDE

One of my favorite *SWAG Letter* stories involves a woman I never even got to meet. I was walking my children to school, and she was talking about an issue of *The SWAG Letter* with someone else on a street corner as we were waiting to cross. She had no idea who I was, and I didn't enlighten her. It was obvious from her head scarf that she was disguising some heavy-duty medical treatment. I overheard her tell the other woman that she was "saving" her *SWAG Letter* to read during a treatment. Well, of course, I sobbed all the way home. That was the most humbling and rewarding moment I have ever experienced as a writer. To provide a few minutes of distraction for someone in that position is my greatest writing accomplishment.

SWAG and *The SWAG Life* are books about women like me—Southern women aging gracefully. In the South, we have a unique sense of humor that allows us to poke fun at ourselves. Luckily, this humor translates well to others living outside the region. There is much to be exalted in the most ordinary events of life, and these books give a new-millennium voice to aspects of our lives that are often viewed as too boring to merit attention. After all, there is no greater joy than regular life being lived full-speed ahead!

These books won't raise your consciousness about a new social ill. They won't make you look younger or skinnier, and they won't improve your stock portfolio. They will, however, provide you with a few hours of pure pleasure and guilt-free, nonfattening fun. I am proud to be a Southern woman, and I am aging as gracefully as I can without any outright sweating.